Basic Milestones
Englisch berufsübergreifend

von
Dr. Wolfgang Schäfer (Hrsg.)
Annely Humphreys
Jason Humphreys
Mary Schäfer

Ernst Klett Verlag
Stuttgart · Leipzig

Basic Milestones

Englisch berufsübergreifend

Autoren: Dr. Wolfgang Schäfer (Hrsg.), Annely Humphreys, Jason Humphreys, Mary Schäfer

Werkübersicht:
Schülerbuch, 978-3-12-808288-2
Milestones Workbook für alle technischen Fachbände mit Prüfungsvorbereitung KMK-Fremdsprachenzertifikat und CD-ROM, Übungsbegleitheft für alle technischen Berufe, 978-3-12-808285-1
Milestones Lehrerhandbuch für technische Berufe inkl. Digitalem Lehrer-Service mit Medien-DVD-ROM + Lehrer-Audio-CDs (6), 978-3-12-808287-5

1. Auflage 1 7 6 5 4 3 | 23 22 21 20 19

Alle Drucke dieser Auflage sind unverändert und können im Unterricht nebeneinander verwendet werden.
Die letzte Zahl bezeichnet das Jahr des Druckes.
Das Werk und seine Teile sind urheberrechtlich geschützt. Jede Nutzung in anderen als den gesetzlich zugelassenen Fällen bedarf der vorherigen schriftlichen Einwilligung des Verlages. Hinweis § 52 a UrhG: Weder das Werk noch seine Teile dürfen ohne eine solche Einwilligung eingescannt und in ein Netzwerk eingestellt werden. Dies gilt auch für Intranets von Schulen und sonstigen Bildungseinrichtungen. Fotomechanische oder andere Wiedergabeverfahren nur mit Genehmigung des Verlages.
Im Lehrwerk befinden sich ausschließlich fiktive Internet-Adressen, die deshalb auch mit ww#. beginnen anstatt wie üblich mit www.
Die im Buch abgedruckten Mediencodes führen zu interaktiven Zusatzübungen und Hörverständnistexten auf www.klett.de. Die Mediencodes leiten ausschließlich zu optionalen Unterrichtsmaterialien, sie unterliegen nicht dem staatlichen Zulassungsverfahren.

© Ernst Klett Verlag GmbH, Stuttgart 2013. Alle Rechte vorbehalten. www.klett.de

Projektleitung: Matthias Rupp
Redaktion: Volker Wendland
Herstellung: Angelika Lindner

Satz und Gestaltung: Satzkiste, Stuttgart
Umschlaggestaltung: Projektteam des Verlages
Reproduktion: Meyle + Müller Medien-Management, Pforzheim
Druck: Druckhaus Götz GmbH, Ludwigsburg

Printed in Germany
ISBN 978-3-12-808288-2

Vorwort

Basic Milestones bietet Ihnen praxisorientiertes berufsübergreifendes Englisch für Berufsschulen, Berufsfachschulen, Fachschulen sowie für Englischkurse in der Erwachsenenbildung.

Basic Milestones im Überblick:

- Konsequente Berücksichtigung neuester Lehrpläne (Lernfelder) sowie durchgängiges Sprachkompetenztraining nach dem Gemeinsamen Europäischen Referenzrahmen (Sprachstufen A2 – B1)
- 8 kompakte 4-seitige Module mit dem Schwerpunkt auf der beruflichen Kommunikation
- Schnelle Orientierung im Buch durch Übersicht der Lernziele jeweils am Modulanfang
- Kompetenzen auf einen Blick: Viele Aufgaben zur Vorbereitung auf die Anforderungen des KMK-Zertifikats (mit den Kürzeln R (Rezeption), P (Produktion), I (Interaktion) und M (Mediation) gekennzeichnet)
- Typische Sprachhandlungssituationen im Berufsalltag: multimedial mit Audio- und Videounterstützung (u. a. Originalvideos der BBC) trainiert
- Zahlreiche Partner-, Gruppen- und Internetaufgaben
- Hilfreiche Verweise auf die nach beruflichen Situationen geordneten Redewendungen *(Phrases)* in den Modulen
- Aufgaben zur Vorbereitung auf das KMK-Fremdsprachenzertifikat in verschiedenen Stufen
- Direkter Zugriff auf den Fachwortschatz in den jeweiligen Modulen über die *Word Bank* (auf jeder Doppelseite)
- Online-Grammatiktraining über die Milestones-Codes ⊕ 3u5mw9 in den Modulen A – H
- Vertieftes Grammatik- und Hörverstehenstraining im Workbook mit Prüfungsvorbereitung auf das KMK-Fremdsprachenzertifikat inklusive CD-ROM mit allen technischen Milestones-Fachbänden- und Workbook-Audios (MP3)

Weiterführendes Material

Milestones Workbook für alle technischen Fachbände mit Prüfungsvorbereitung KMK-Fremdsprachenzertifikat und CD-ROM

Lehrerhandbuch für alle technischen Milestones-Fachbände mit 6 Audio-CDs + Digitaler Lehrer-Service (Lehrer-Software mit multimedialen Schülerbüchern, Audios, Videos, Lösungen, Übungsmaterial, Übungsgenerator, Dokumentenpool mit veränderbaren Materialien)

Inhalt

1 | Meeting people — 8

TOPICS Introducing and greeting
Intercultural awareness
AUDIOS ⊙ A 1.1
KMK-AUFGABEN Mediation, Stufe II
▶ Workbook

2 | Your company — 12

TOPICS The company and its departments
Tasks and responsibilities
Organisational structure
AUDIOS ⊙ A 1.2
KMK-AUFGABEN Mediation / Produktion, Stufe II
▶ Workbook

3 | Telephoning — 16

TOPICS Making and receiving a phone call
Giving information over the phone
AUDIOS ⊙ A 1.3
KMK-AUFGABEN Interaktion / Rezeption, Stufe I
▶ Workbook

4 | Written communication — 20

TOPICS Enquiries
Offers
Orders
KMK-AUFGABEN Mediation, Stufe II
▶ Workbook

5 | Applications · 24

TOPICS Job advertisements
Letter of application
CV
AUDIOS A 1.4
KMK-AUFGABEN Mediation / Rezeption / Produktion, Stufe I / II / II
▶ Workbook

6 | Socialising · 28

TOPICS Small talk
Eating out
AUDIOS A 1.5
KMK-AUFGABEN Rezeption / Mediation, Stufe II
▶ Workbook

7 | Presentations · 32

TOPICS Preparing and delivering a presentation
Describing materials and products
AUDIOS A 1.6
KMK-AUFGABEN Mediation, Stufe I / II
▶ Workbook

8 | Dealing with customers · 36

TOPICS Complaints
Customer service
AUDIOS A 1.7
KMK-AUFGABEN Rezeption, Stufe II
▶ Workbook

Video lounge (Die Videos und die Videoskripte befinden sich im Lehrerhandbuch.)

V 1 Company tour

V 2 Telephoning

V 3 Job interview

V 4 Technical support

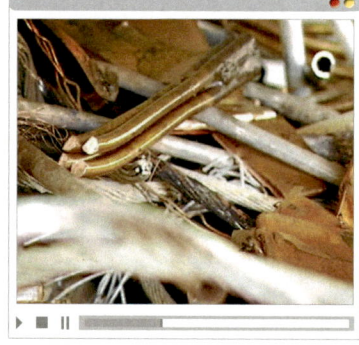
V 5 Waste – the future's most valuable resource

V 6 Pipe inspection

V 7 High voltage work

V 8 Ras Laffan

V 9 Pipelines

V 10 Robots in the hospital

V 11 Portable power stations

V 12 Car speed control

Appendix

KMK-Prüfungssatz Stufe I	46
Role cards	49
Phrases	50
Audio / Video scripts	61
Grammar overview	73
Chronological word list	85
Alphabetical word list	90
Further reading	93
Maps United Kingdom, USA	95

Umschlagseiten

Classroom phrases	I
Irregular verbs	II
Shapes	III
Mathematical terms and symbols; Conversion table	IV

🌐 Üben interaktiv: Online Grammatiktraining

Modul 1: 3u5mw9	**Modul 3:** x3gj95	**Modul 5:** 5zw8jx	**Modul 7:** 3b9c4h
Modul 2: gc2x9w	**Modul 4:** cy8yn5	**Modul 6:** pf5r3n	**Modul 8:** 842j42

Modulelemente

Nach diesem Modul	Lernziele
WORD BANK	Fachvokabular
→ **PHRASES:** Telephoning	Verweis auf Phrases (Telephoning) im Anhang

---

Symbole

⊙ A 1.27	Audioverweis mit Tracknummer (CD1 – Track 27)
P, M, I, R	Produktion, Mediation, Interaktion, Rezeption
🌐	Aufgabe mit Internetrecherche
👥	Partner- und Gruppenaufgaben
🌐 3u5mw9	Grammatiktraining online über www.klett.de
KMK II	Aufgabe zur Vorbereitung auf die Prüfung des KMK-Fremdsprachenzertifikats (Niveaustufe II)

Module 1 | Meeting people

3u5mw9

1

NACH DIESEM MODUL:

√ weiß ich, wie man sich auf Englisch begrüßt,

√ weiß ich, wie ich mich selbst und andere einander auf Englisch vorstelle.

Meeting people

In the world of work you will often meet new people and it will be necessary to introduce yourself. In all industries developing relationships with colleagues and customers is the key to success. Not only is it important that you are polite, confident and friendly, but also that you know what to say, what information to include, and what the differences between formal and informal situations are.

1 Match the parts of the dialogues to form short conversations. Start with Speaker A.

Speaker A	Speaker B
1. Morning, Tom. That was a great game last night, wasn't it?	a. Nice to meet you, too, Hannah.
2. Hi guys, my name's Natalie.	b. Goodbye, Mr Horvath. It was nice meeting you.
3. Goodbye, Mr Bauer. See you next week.	c. Morning Chris. Yeah, it was amazing!
4. It's nice to meet you, Simon.	d. Hi Natalie, I'm Michael. Welcome to the team.

2 Now match the conversations above with the appropriate picture (1–4) and decide which are formal and which are informal.

P **3** Which other phrases do you know for greeting somebody and saying goodbye? Make a list.

A | Saying "hello" and "goodbye" and giving your name

A trainee from Denmark has just arrived at Neureuther und Söhne in Kiel for a three-month internship.

R **1**
⊙ A 1.1   Listen to the two dialogues and write down the names of the people and their positions in the company.

R **2**
⊙ A 1.1   Listen again and write down the phrases the people use for greeting and introducing one another.

R **3**   Match the replies to the greetings and goodbyes in the two boxes.

Formal greetings/goodbyes	Formal replies
1. Good morning. How are you today?	a. Good morning. I'm fine, thanks. And you?
2. Good night. Have a nice evening, Mr Dachs.	b. Goodbye, Mr Schäfer, and thanks for everything.
3. Goodbye, Mr Horvath. Have a nice journey home.	c. Good night, Ms Kistner, you too.
4. Good night, Silke.	d. Good night, Ms Hornbach.

Informal greetings/goodbyes	Informal replies
1. Hello, Mike. Haven't seen you for a long time.	a. Bye, Thomas. Give me a call, will you?
2. Lena, how are you this morning?	b. You, too, Florian. Thank you.
3. Morning. How was your weekend?	c. Fine, thanks. How about yours?
4. Bye-bye, Sevda.	d. I'm good, thanks. Yourself?
5. Have a nice weekend, Joe.	e. Yes, I was away on a trip last week.

P **4**   Make dialogues from the following prompts and present them to the class.
Look at your lists of phrases from exercise 2 and check the info box on the next page.

Example:
A: Hello, my name is Marina Kohler. I represent Toolcell in Leipzig.
B: Hello, Ms Kohler. I'm Amy Strong from Easytools in Bern. Nice to meet you.
A: Nice to meet you, too, Ms Strong.

Names: Denise Hofmann • Marina Kohler • Alice Campbell • Abel Kazich • Tanja Neuhäuser • Rudolfo Orvieto • Ursula Braun • Stefan Helm • Gerard Mathieu • your name

Job descriptions: I'm a trainee/intern • I work for … • I come from … • I represent … • I'm training to be a … • your job

Companies: Toolcell GmbH in Leipzig, Germany • Easytools in Bern, Switzerland • Tools Expert Pontypridd, Wales • DWT Electronics, Stuttgart • Smart EDV, Kiel • Xiang Piong Ltd, Hong Kong • Naturholz GmbH • your company

Situations: a first meeting with a new customer • a meeting with an existing customer/a colleague • a party • a company open day • a trade fair • a job fair for trainees • the first day in a new company

WORD BANK ⊙

intern – Praktikant(in)

Module 1 | Meeting people

5 **Introduce the people to each other according to the following structure.**
Use the prompts on the previous page.

→ **PHRASES:** Meeting people

A: Fragen Sie **B** und **C**, ob sie sich schon kennen. **B** und **C** antworten mit Nein.
A: Stellen Sie **B** und **C** einander vor.

B: Begrüßen Sie **C** freundlich.

C: Sie grüßen **B** zurück und stellen eine Frage zu **B**s Firma

B: Sie geben eine Auskunft über Ihre Firma. Sie fragen **C** nach seiner Tätigkeit.

C: Sie beantworten **B**s Frage.

INFO BOX: Meeting people

First meeting / Formal introduction
A: Hello, my name is Ines Sacher.
B: Nice to meet you, Ms Sacher. My name is Joshua Hamsung.
A: Nice to meet you, too, Mr Hamsung.
Women – married or not – are addressed as Ms, not Miss.

A: Mr Jacobs, this is Mr Sykes.
B: How do you do?
C: How do you do?
"How do you do?" is rarely used for first introductions.

A: I'm Frank Warren of Wood Tools in Manchester.
   Please call me Frank.
B: Pleased to meet you, Frank. My name is Joanne McNeill.
   Do call me Joanne.
In English-speaking countries first names are often used from the start of a business realtionship. In South America or Asia, however, you don't usually use first names right away.

I hope you had a good trip. /
I hope you had no trouble finding us. /
Welcome to our stand.
Phrases like these are used to break the ice after an introduction.

Second meeting
A: Good morning, Ms Sacher. Do you remember me?
   I'm Joshua Hamsung from Bell & Co in Chicago.
B: Good morning, Mr Hamsung. Nice to see you again.

Informal meetings
A: Hello Ines. Great to see you again. How are you?
B: Hi Joshua. Lovely to see you, too. I'm fine. And you?

B | Intercultural awareness

 1 **Ihr Betrieb wird in Zukunft für einen amerikanischen Auftraggeber arbeiten. Ihre Vorgesetzte interessiert sich daher für folgenden Artikel aus einer englischen Fachzeitschrift. Sie bittet Sie, die wesentlichen Aussagen des Artikels stichpunktartig in übersichtlicher Form für sie auf Deutsch herauszuarbeiten.**

Intercultural awareness
Politeness, pleasantries and profitability

Americans are known to be direct, but they do like to take a few minutes to chat before getting down to work. They may ask after your health, or if your trip was pleasant, or about where you are from. This gives both parties a chance to form an impression of the other and establishes a basis on which to do business.

Americans, including the president, like to be called by their given name. This is not an invitation to be personal, as you would expect in Germany if someone suggested using the familiar "Du". It is a way to set a framework for working together. While it is usual in business, it would not be expected in dealing with a doctor, a teacher or a professor, and in any case, you should wait until it is offered: "Hello, I'm James Smith, vice-president in charge of sales. Call me Jim." "Pleased to meet you! I'm Walter König; please call me Walter." (Note that in the United States you state your *given* name and then your *family* name, and not the other way around, except perhaps on a form that you have to fill out.)

Americans don't like to waste time. They get to the point, in conversations as well as in conferences. Although Milton Berle, a comedian from the 1950s and 1960s, is quoted as saying: "A committee is a group of people that keeps minutes and wastes hours."

Americans are generally very polite, and they tend to smile much more than we are used to. An American tourist was quite upset that perfect strangers didn't smile back at her when she walked through the streets of a small town in Germany. On the other hand, a German woman in New York became quite tired of being asked, again by perfect strangers, the person at the cash register, the bus driver: "How are you doing?" and commanded to "Have a nice day!" These pleasantries are intended to show that you are noticed and respected. More than "Thanks!" is not expected.

 2 **Check the Internet to see what advice people from other countries get to prepare for meetings in Germany. Make a list of ten useful tips.**

Module 2 | Your company

2

NACH DIESEM MODUL:

√ kann ich verschiedene Firmenabteilungen auf Englisch erklären,

√ kann ich Arbeitsplätze und Tätigkeiten auf Englisch beschreiben,

√ kann ich eine Firmenstruktur auf Englisch beschreiben.

Your company

Regardless of whether your company builds houses, bakes bread, or makes furniture, there is likely to come a time where you will be required to talk about yourself, your job and your company in English. Whether you are greeting an English-speaking visitor, giving a tour of the factory, or talking to suppliers from another country, it is important you have the skills and vocabulary to express yourself clearly.

1 Work on your own. Look at the photos and brainstorm words that describe what is shown in each of them.

I/P 2 Compare your list of words with your partner and work together to describe the pictures. Use these words to help you:

> bakery • kitchen • dough • gardener • bush • pruning • overalls • wellington boots • pallet truck • shelving • storage • tool box • tools • repair

WATCH OUT!
He ~~wears~~ overalls.   He is wearing overalls.

P 3 With your partner, think of three questions you would like to ask each of the four young workers shown in the photos.

A | The company and its departments

1 Use the words and phrases in the table to explain what the departments of Krone Elektronik GmbH do.

Example: Sales and Marketing advertises and sells the products.

Department		
Sales and Marketing	distribute	the products are not damaged.
Production Planning	advertise and sell	new employees.
Accounts	check	raw materials.
HR (Human Resources)	buy	the products.
Production	deal with	the computer network.
Logistics	recruit and train	the finished products.
Purchasing	maintain	customer problems.
Customer Service	handle	the company's finances.
R&D (Research and Development)	make	new products.
IT (Information Technology)	organize	production schedules.
Quality Control	develop	the products to the customers.

2 Use the information in the table to form sentences using *responsible for / in charge of*.

Example:
The Production department is responsible for making the products.
The Production Planning department is in charge of …

3 Look at the departments again and write down three questions. Then close your book and ask your partner.

Example:
A: What is the Quality Control department responsible for?
B: It is responsible for …
A: Which department is in charge of …?
B: The … department is in charge of …

4 Der Ausbildungsleiter von Krone Elektronik, Herr Kirchner, zeigt Sean, einem Elektrotechnikstudenten aus Belfast, das Firmengelände und die einzelnen Abteilungen. Hören Sie sich das Gespräch an und beantworten Sie die folgenden Fragen auf Deutsch.

1. Wann wurde Krone Elektronik GmbH gegründet, und von wem?
2. Wo hat die Firma ihren Hauptsitz?
3. Wie viele Produktionsanlagen hat Krone Elektronik insgesamt?
4. Wo wird nächstes Jahr eine neue Produktionsanlage eröffnet?
5. Wie viele Leute beschäftigt die Firma?
6. Woran arbeitet die Forschungs- und Entwicklungsabteilung gerade?
7. Welche drei Abteilungen befinden sich in dem Hauptgebäude?
8. Wo wird Sean zuerst arbeiten?
9. Wie viele Zylinderköpfe werden jährlich bei Krone Elektronik hergestellt?
10. Was passiert momentan in der IT-Abteilung?

WORD BANK

bush – Busch
dough – Teig
pallet truck – Handhubwagen
prune (v) – beschneiden
raw materials – Rohmaterialien
recruit (v) – anwerben

Module 2 | Your company

B | Tasks and responsibilities

Industrial companies are made up of many different people, who all have a variety of tasks and responsibilities. DWG Tech GmbH in Stuttgart manufactures machine parts for the automotive and aviation industry. Below, Tim Schieber, a DWG Tech GmbH employee, talks about his job and daily activities on DWG Tech GmbH's English website.

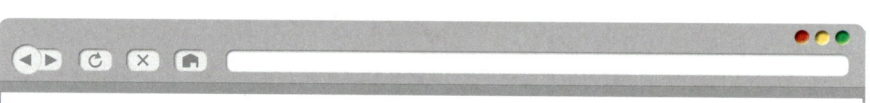

R 1 Read the text and answer the following questions in your own words.

1. What do CNC machines do?
2. What problems can occur with CNC machines?

Hi, my name is Tim Schieber and I work as a CNC machine operator here at the DWG Tech headquarters in Stuttgart. I've been with the company since completing my apprenticeship three years ago and next summer I am going to work at the DWG Tech branch in Detroit.

5 In my opinion, what we do here is very important. CNC is all about precision, and it is therefore essential that I concentrate at all times. These machines drill, shape, cut and polish the parts for automobiles and aeroplanes. As a CNC machine operator I am responsible for one machine. As I said, this job is all about precision, and the machines are programmed specifically for each job. I do not do the programming
10 myself, but I learnt programming during my apprenticeship and I sometimes have to intervene when something goes wrong – such as a vibrating workpiece or broken cutting tools.

The CNC process is almost entirely automatic. It is my job to set up the machine for the production process, which means loading the machine with the correct tools and
15 workpieces. Once the programming for an operation is done, I enter the commands into the machine. To do this we use a computer network. The next step is to let the machine work its magic.

The main part of my job is to monitor the machine and spot problems. This means checking that the machine is running smoothly, measuring finished workpieces to
20 check that the dimensions are correct, and sometimes replacing tools. It is also important that the machine is kept cool and lubricated with a special lubricating oil – but this is also done automatically. Of course, another of my tasks is to make sure the machine is kept clean, and that the working area is safe.

My working day depends on what shift I am on. We generally work either early shift
25 or late shift. Early shift is from 6am until 2pm, and the guys on late shift begin at 2pm and clock out at 10pm. Sometimes, if we have a lot of work to do, there is also a night shift – but that doesn't happen too often. I actually prefer early shift. Even though I don't enjoy waking up at 4:45am, it is great to have the afternoon to do whatever I like – especially in the summer.

30 I really enjoy my job and I am proud to be working for an international company like DWG. My colleagues and I are always very busy and it can be fairly stressful. But I love working with the machines and it is interesting to see the many technological developments in the industry.

---

2 Find the synonyms in the text for the following words:

1. to finish
2. very important
3. cars
4. accuracy
5. to observe
6. usually
7. to like
8. workmates
9. quite

14

R **3** **Decide whether the statements are true or false. Give reasons for your decisions in German.**

1. Tim is currently doing an apprenticeship as a CNC machine operator.
2. Once the machine starts running, Tim's work is over.
3. One of Tim's tasks is making sure that the cutting tools are not broken.
4. Tim rarely works in shifts.
5. Accuracy is very important for CNC work.
6. The technology used in CNC machining has hardly changed over the years.

P **4** **Your boss has asked you to write a short text for your company's English website. Make sure you include some basic facts about your company and details about your daily tasks and responsibilities. Use some of the phrases in Tim's text, e.g.** *I work as, I've been with the company since***, etc.**

→ **PHRASES:** Your company

P/I **5** **Check the Internet for a job in your industry that interests you. Make notes on the daily tasks and responsibilities.**

I **6** **Explain the job you researched to your partner, but don't mention the job title. Your partner must guess what the job is from the description you give. Then swap roles.**

C | Organisational structure

P/M **KMK II** Sie sind Auszubildende(r) in der DWG Tech GmbH. Ihr Vorgesetzter benötigt eine Übersicht über die Ingenieursabteilung der DWG Tech GmbH Niederlassung in Detroit. Auf deren Firmen-Homepage finden Sie die folgenden Informationen zu den Mitarbeitern. Zeichnen Sie ein Organigramm nach der vorliegenden Beschreibung.

Who's who in DWG Tech GmbH Detroit's engineering department?

DWG Tech GmbH Inc. employs around 60 people in its engineering department. The department is led by Chief Engineer Dr. Adam Foster, who is supported by his Personal Assistant Helen Green and DWG Tech's Assistant Chief Engineer Dr. Tim Bayliss. The engineering department is split into two core areas: automotive and aviation. Shift leaders Chris Falsone and Sandra Borowski report to Michael Kellermann, the foreman. They all belong to automotive which is run by experienced Chief Automotive Engineer, Dr. Torben Brinkema. DWG Tech's aviation department is in the capable hands of Dr. Judith Sommer, Chief Aviation Engineer, who has been with the company for over 15 years. Dr. Sommer is supported by foreman Frank Kapowski. Barry Richardson and Jens Schmelzer are the two shift leaders and work closely with Mr Kapowski.

WORD BANK

aviation – Luftfahrt
CNC (computerized numerical control) – CNC (computerisierte numerische Steuerung)
dimensions – Maße
drill (v) – bohren
lubricated – geölt
lubricating oil – Schmieröl
measure (v) – messen
polish (v) – schleifen, polieren
precision – Genauigkeit
shape (v) – fräsen, formen
vibrate (v) – vibrieren
workpiece – Werkstück

WORD BANK ⊙

braking system – Bremsanlage
cylinder head – Zylinderkopf
interface – Schnittstelle
manufacturing plant – Produktionsbetrieb
operating system – Betriebssystem

Module 3 | Telephoning

NACH DIESEM MODUL:

√ kenne ich die wichtigsten Redewendungen um ein Telefongespräch zu führen,

√ kann ich Maße, Namen und Adressen am Telefon auf Englisch weitergeben.

Telephoning

When you are on the job, chances are you will have your mobile phone with you – it does not matter what line of work you are in. Whether you are landscaping a garden, fixing a leak, or installing a telephone line, your phone can ring at any time. It could be a customer with a complaint, you may have to ring a supplier or check the status of an order. And if you have to talk in English, you need to have the necessary skills to understand and be understood, no matter what the situation.

P 1 Look at the photos. What might the people be talking about on the telephone? Compare your answers with a partner. Use these words to help you:

> materials • problem • delay • support • help • breakdown • repair • solution • angry • confused • crash • computer network room

2 Match the German words below with the English equivalents.

1. Handy	a. message
2. Anrufbeantworter	b. hands-free device
3. Festnetz	c. extension number
4. Nachricht	d. mobile/cell phone
5. Durchwahl	e. answering machine
6. Freisprechanlage	f. area code
7. Vorwahl	g. country code
8. Ländervorwahl	h. landline

A | Making and receiving a phone call

R 1 Which of the following phrases are used for making calls and which ones for receiving calls? Make a list.

1. Could you put me through to Mr Warren, please?
2. I'm sorry, but Mr/Ms … is in a meeting at the moment.
3. How can I help you?
4. Thank you. I'll ring back later.
5. Can I ask what your call is about?
6. Would you like to leave a message?
7. Thank you very much for your help.
8. My name is Barry Potter and I'm calling from …
9. May I take your name, please?
10. I'd like to speak to somebody in the production department, please.
11. Hold the line, please. I'll put you through.
12. Could you tell him/her that …?

M 2 Read the telephone conversation below and find the English equivalents for the following German expressions.

→ **PHRASES:** Telephoning

1. Haben Sie etwas zum Schreiben?
2. Soll ich Ihnen seine Handynummer geben?
3. Er ist leider zurzeit nicht im Büro.
4. Ich hätte gerne mit … gesprochen.
5. Einen Moment, bitte.
6. Wie kann ich Ihnen helfen?

Christoph:	Landschaftsgärtnerei Brock, Christoph Fink.
Caller:	Er, yes, hello. Do you speak English?
Christoph:	Certainly. How can I help you?
Caller:	This is Landschaftsgärtnerei Brock in Kiel, isn't it?
Christoph:	Yes, that's correct.
Caller:	Great. My name is Erik Pedersen and I'm calling from Danske Onlinebank Copenhagen. I'd like to speak to Mr Gebhardt, please.
Christoph:	Sorry, but Mr Gebhardt is not in the office at the moment. Can I take a message, or would you like his mobile number?
Caller:	Can you give me his mobile number, please?
Christoph:	Ok, do you have a pen?
Caller:	Just a second, please … ok, go ahead.
Christoph:	The number is 0049-170 557624.
Caller:	Sorry, I didn't catch that. Could you speak up a bit?
Christoph:	Yes, of course. The number is 0049-170 557624.
Caller:	Thank you very much.
Christoph:	You're welcome. Maybe you can give me your phone number.
Caller:	Certainly. It's 0045, that's the country code for Denmark, 32, the area code for Copenhagen, and then 54 58 11. Oh, and my extension number is 944.
Christoph:	0045-32 54 58 11, extension 944. Thank you very much. Goodbye.
Caller:	Goodbye.

WORD BANK

breakdown – Störung, Ausfall
crash – Absturz
leak – Leck

Module 3 | Telephoning

> **INTERCULTURAL BOX**
>
> **Intercultural awareness – Telephoning in English-speaking countries**
> When talking on the phone in English it is important that you use suitable and polite phrases. For example, if you know the person you are calling, it is common to make a little small talk before getting down to business. One thing to remember: Although it is common for English people to quickly switch to first names, it is still important to remain polite and remember that you are talking to a customer or a colleague, and not your best friend.
> **Example:** *How are you? I haven't spoken to you for a while.*
> If you have to give bad news or talk about a problem, then you should begin with *I'm afraid …* or *Unfortunately …* .
> **Example:** *I'm afraid we cannot install your wireless internet connection this week.*
> A request often begins with *Could you possibly …* or *I would be grateful if you would / could …* .
> **Example:** *I would be grateful if you would call me back later.*
> When someone thanks you for your help, or for a job well done, you can simply say *You're welcome*. And be careful! Whereas in German, just saying *yes* or *no* may be fine, this is considered to be quite impolite in England. Instead, just say *Yes, I think so*, or *No, I'm afraid not*. If you call somebody, you should give your name, where you are calling from, and say who you would like to speak to.
> **Example:** *Hello, my name is Felix Hirschbach, calling from Crown Electronics. Could I speak to Ms Cameron, please?*

P **3** How would you say the following things more politely?

 → **PHRASES:** Telephoning

1. Eh? Say it again!
2. Give me your number!
3. What do you want?
4. What's your name?
5. I can't hear you!
6. What?
7. He's not here!
8. Give me Ms Bauer!

I **4** Sie arbeiten im International Calls Service Center der Landschaftsgärtnerei Brock in Kiel und erhalten einen Anruf. Führen Sie das folgende Telefongespräch mit einem Partner auf Englisch.

Landschaftsgärtnerei Brock, Kiel.	Stefanie Berg, dänische Kundin
Nehmen Sie den Anruf entgegen.	Nennen Sie Ihren Namen. Sie möchten mit Herrn Gebhardt sprechen.
Sagen Sie, dass Sie die Anruferin schlecht verstehen und bitten Sie sie, etwas lauter zu sprechen.	Sprechen Sie etwas lauter und fragen Sie, ob Sie jetzt besser zu verstehen sind.
Bejahen Sie und fragen Sie, worum es geht.	Erklären Sie, dass Ihre Firma ein neues Bürogebäude gebaut hat und Sie möchten, dass Firma Brock den Gartenbereich gestaltet. Sie haben ein Angebot erhalten und möchten mit Herrn Gebhardt darüber sprechen.
Sagen Sie, dass es Ihnen leid tut und dass Herr Gebhardt momentan bei einem Kunden ist. Er wird sich melden, sobald er zurück ist. Es sollte nicht lange dauern. Fragen Sie, ob Herr Gebhardt Ihre Telefonnummer bereits hat.	Bejahen Sie. Bedanken Sie sich und beenden Sie das Gespräch.
Bedanken Sie sich auch und verabschieden Sie sich.	

B | Giving information over the phone

Making a quick call is often the fastest and easiest way of passing on valuable information, such as measurements or figures. However, misunderstandings can happen very quickly, so it is important to make sure any information is delivered clearly and correctly.

1 Match the English word to the German translation.

1. height	a. Breite
2. length	b. Gewicht
3. width	c. Höhe
4. weight	d. Tiefe
5. depth	e. Länge

INFO BOX: Saying weights and measurements

nine **point** five milimetres (9.5 mm)   100 **by** 30 **by** 15 (100 x 30 x 15)
thirty one **square** metres (31 m²)   twenty **cubic** metres (20 m³)
one **point** two five litre engine (1.25 l)   6000 revolutions **per** minute (6000 rpm)
170 kilometers **per** hour (170 kph)   two hundred **and** twenty volts (220 V)

2 What are the adjectives for the nouns in exercise 1?

3 Sit back to back with a partner. Take turns in giving each other different information over the phone. Partner A uses role card A, Partner B uses role card B (see Appendix).

4 Sit back to back and spell your name, the name and address of your company, and your email address. Use the table below to help you.

Symbol	Name	Example
@	at	info@
B / b	capital letter / lower case	NYC / asap
-	hyphen / dash	t-online
ö	o-umlaut / oe / o with two dots	Schönberg
:	colon	http:
/	slash / stroke / forward slash	org/news
\	backslash	\docs
.	dot	.de
_	underscore	customer_info

5 Alex Bauder works for Fertighaus Henke in Magdeburg and is called by Mr Reid, an English customer who lives in Germany and who is currently building a house near Magdeburg. Listen to the conversation and answer the following questions.

1. Who is Mr Deschler?
2. Why can't Mr Reid speak to him personally?
3. Why does Mr Reid want to speak to Mr Deschler?
4. When will Fertighaus Henke begin building Mr Reid's cellar?
5. Why does the extractor fan need to be moved to the left?
6. Which changes is Mr Deschler not responsible for?
7. What should Mr Deschler do next?

WORD BANK

cubic metre – Kubikmeter
revolutions per minute – Drehzahl
socket – Steckdose
square metre – Quadratmeter

WORD BANK ⊙

construction manager – Bauleiter
diameter – Durchmesser
extractor fan – Dunstabzugshaube
foundation pit – Baugrube
hob – Kochfeld

6 Now listen to the conversation again and make notes of the changes Mr Reid wants, where he wants them, and details about the measurements, where given.

Module 4 | Written communication

4

NACH DIESEM MODUL:

✓ kann ich auf Englisch kurze Anfragen, Angebote und Bestellungen als Brief, E-Mail oder Fax erstellen,

✓ kann ich englische Briefe, E-Mails und Faxe beantworten.

Written communication

Written communication such as emails, faxes and business letters play an essential role in business, both in the office and the workshop. For any company to run efficiently, it is necessary to have an effective communication system – making sure that enquiries are answered promptly, offers are made on time, and orders are placed and processed correctly. The standard business letter has been replaced in recent years by the faster email, and to a lesser extent, the fax. In all areas of business today it is common to have dealings with countries across the globe, meaning you need to be able to understand written communication in English.

P **1** Look at the pictures above and describe them in your own words.

P **2** What are the advantages and disadvantages of the forms of written communication shown in the pictures? Create a list. Use these words to help you:

> confidential · instant · easy · time-consuming · reliable · signal · misunderstanding · slow · personal · formal · informal

3 Compare your lists with a partner and come up with a final list for each form of communication. Share your final list with the class.

A | Enquiries

Business transactions generally begin with an enquiry. For example, a private customer is looking for a caterer for a wedding, or a farm is looking for new equipment.

M 1 George Wright, who runs a farm in East Sussex, is interested in buying some agricultural equipment from Landwirtschaftswelt AG in Hannover. Read George's enquiry and sum up the main information in German.

Dear Sir/Madam,

Agricultural equipment supplier

We recently visited your website and were very impressed with your range of agricultural equipment.

We are a family-run farm in East Sussex, England with over 30 employees.

We are currently looking for a new supplier of farming and agricultural equipment and are interested in your products. Therefore we would ask you to send us a copy of your latest catalogue and price list.

Please also inform us about your export prices and possible discounts as well as terms of payment and delivery and delivery times.

We would also appreciate it if you could send us information you have on any used agricultural equipment you have available.

Thank you for your attention to this enquiry and we look forward to hearing from you.

Yours sincerely,

a. appropriate salutation
b. subject line
c. source of address
d. introduction of your firm
e. reason for enquiry
f. request to send catalogue and price list
g. request for information on prices and discounts and terms of payment and delivery
h. further requests
i. closing phrase
j. complimentary close

R 2 Match these parts of an enquiry with the descriptions (a. – j.) above.

1. Best wishes.
2. Your company was recommended to me by a colleague.
3. We are a large production company, specialising in machine components.
4. Please let us have a detailed cost estimate for configuring our IT network.
5. We hope to hear from you soon.
6. What are your terms of payment for regular customers?
7. As we are convinced that your products will sell well on the American market …
8. A visit by your representative would be greatly appreciated.
9. Please let us know whether you can supply from stock.
10. Machine component supplier

WORD BANK

agricultural equipment – landwirtschaftliche Geräte

Module 4 | Written communication

B | Offers

P 1 Read the offer email below and complete it using the words from the box.

> bank transfer · discount · interest · business · working days ·
> attachment · delivery period · stock · orders

From: mailto:t.wolf@landwirtschaftswelt...de **Sent:** 201_-05-30 14:52
To: mailto:info@sussexfarm.co...uk
Cc: mailto:k.mueller@landwirtschaftswelt...de
Subject: Your enquiry

Attachments Hauptkatalog_2012.pdf

Dear Mr Wright

Thank you for your enquiry and your [1] in our products.

We are sending you our latest brochure and price list as an [2].
For [3] of € 10,000 or more we are able to grant a [4] of five per cent.
For large orders (over 20) we require a [5] of 10 – 14 [6].
Smaller orders can be delivered from [7] and within 3 – 5 working days.

Our usual terms of payment are by [8] to our account with the GDB Bank in Gelsenkirchen.

Thank you again for your enquiry. We look forward to establishing regular [9] with you.

Yours sincerely

Tim Wolf

P 2 Use the following notes to write an enquiry and an offer in English.

→ **PHRASES:**
Written communication

Enquiry
(You work at Construct World.)

- large DIY store in Poland (Construct World), looking to buy quality German-made tools
- saw your company (Hauch Werkzeuge KG) at a trade show in Hannover
- would like information about delivery times, discounts, copy of catalogue
- would like some samples to inspect
- polite ending

Angebot
(Sie arbeiten bei Hauch Werkzeuge.)

- Bedanken Sie sich für die Anfrage.
- Gerne schicken Sie Ihren aktuellen Prospekt inklusive Preisliste zu.
- Lieferzeit (nach Polen):
  große Bestellungen (über 500 Stück): 5 – 10 Werktage,
  kleine Bestellungen: 2 – 4 Werktage
- Preisnachlass ab Bestellwert von 2.500 € möglich (5 %)
- Sie würden sich freuen, mit Construct World zusammenarbeiten zu dürfen.
- höflicher Schluss

C | Orders

1 **Read the order fax below and complete it using the prepositions in the box below.**

for (2x) • by • of • to (3x) • with

TELEFAX Message

Sussex Farm
Lewes
East Sussex
BN8 8GZ
Tel.: 0044 (0)1323 554997… • Fax: 0044 (0)1323 554998…

To: Landwirtschaftswelt AG   Attention: Mr Tim Wolf
     Schmiedstrasse 44
     79098 Freiburg   Fax: 0049 761 721965…
     Germany

From: George Wright

Subject: Order

Dear Mr Wolf

Thank you very much **1** your email **2** 30 May.

Thank you also for sending us your catalogue and price list.
We were very impressed **3** your range of agricultural equipment and would like to place an order **4** 2 round balers, item number KJ221, 1 threshing machine, item number WZ330, and 4 balance plows, item number HW438.

Please confirm this order indicating the bank account **5** which you wish to have the sum in question transferred.

Please deliver the goods **6** our farm at Sussex Farm, Lewes, East Sussex, BN8 8GZ.

We look forward **7** receiving the consignment soon and to placing further orders **8** you.

Best regards

G. Wright

George Wright

2 **Sie arbeiten bei der Landwirtschaftswelt AG in Freiburg. Ihr Chef bittet Sie, das obige Fax für ihn auf Deutsch zusammenzufassen, damit er über den Auftrag informiert ist.**

Module 5 | Applications

5zw8jx

5

NACH DIESEM MODUL:

✓ kann ich eine Stellenanzeige auf Englisch verstehen,

✓ kann ich meine Fähigkeiten und Qualifikationen auf Englisch beschreiben,

✓ kann ich eine Bewerbung auf Englisch schreiben.

1 2 3 4

Applications

The world today is full of opportunities. You might decide to work in your hometown, a big city, or even another country. Maybe you want to work for a small family-run company or a major corporation with branches across the globe. Whatever you decide, the opportunities are out there, but it is up to you to take them.

1 Look at the pictures above and describe them using the words below.

> to apply • job advertisement • letter of application • CV • to search •
> job interview • employment contract • to invite • newspaper • to write

2 Put the steps of the application process shown in the pictures above into the correct order.

P **3** Work on your own. What skills and qualifications do you need for a job in your industry? Make a list. Use these words to help you:

> hard-working • motivated • logical • good with food • good with your
> hands • communicative • good team player • able to understand plans
> and diagrams • attention to detail • computer skills • able to work outdoors

4 Work with a partner and decide upon a final list. Share it with the class.

24

A | Job advertisements

M/R 1 Read the three online job advertisements below and find the English translations for the following German words and expressions.

1. verantwortungsbewusst
2. Bewerber
3. kreativ
4. pünktlich
5. lernbereit
6. begeistert
7. gültige Fahrerlaubnis
8. Erfahrung
9. abgeschlossene Ausbildung
10. gute Bezahlung
11. fließendes Englisch
12. hygienisch
13. belastbar
14. freie Stelle

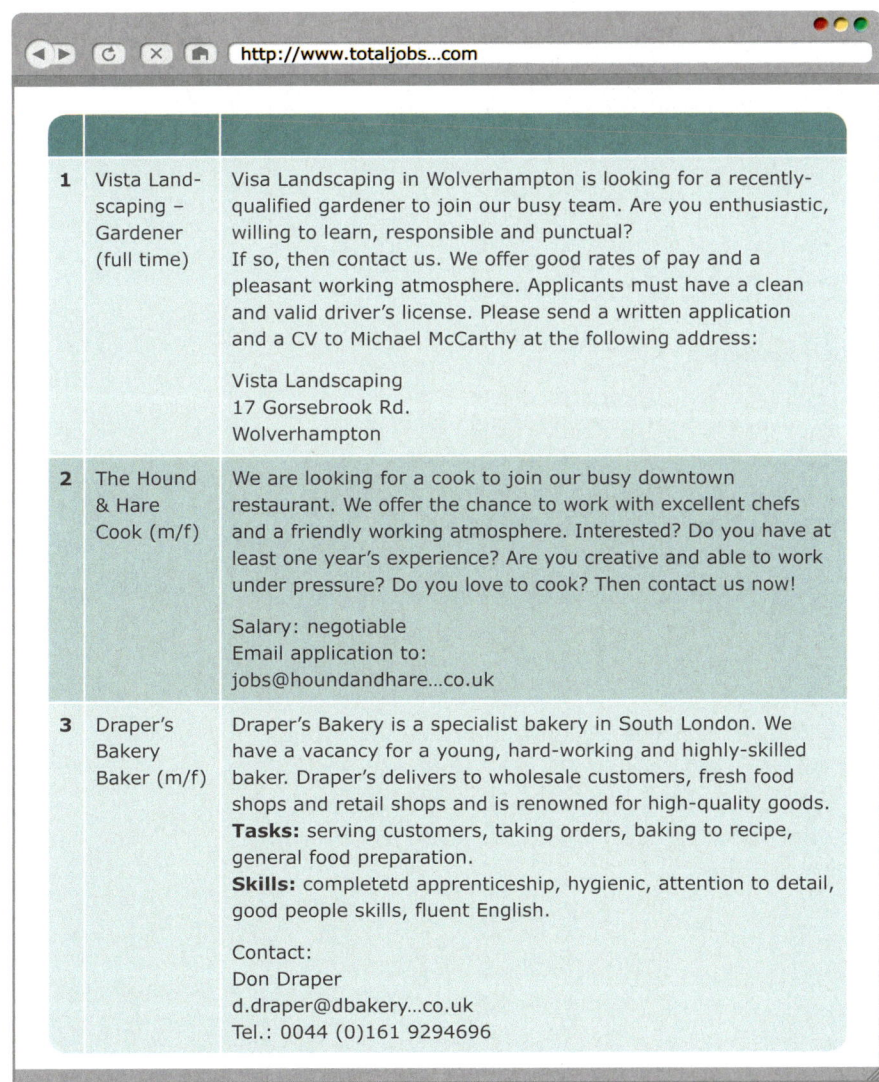

1	Vista Landscaping – Gardener (full time)	Visa Landscaping in Wolverhampton is looking for a recently-qualified gardener to join our busy team. Are you enthusiastic, willing to learn, responsible and punctual? If so, then contact us. We offer good rates of pay and a pleasant working atmosphere. Applicants must have a clean and valid driver's license. Please send a written application and a CV to Michael McCarthy at the following address: Vista Landscaping 17 Gorsebrook Rd. Wolverhampton
2	The Hound & Hare Cook (m/f)	We are looking for a cook to join our busy downtown restaurant. We offer the chance to work with excellent chefs and a friendly working atmosphere. Interested? Do you have at least one year's experience? Are you creative and able to work under pressure? Do you love to cook? Then contact us now! Salary: negotiable Email application to: jobs@houndandhare...co.uk
3	Draper's Bakery Baker (m/f)	Draper's Bakery is a specialist bakery in South London. We have a vacancy for a young, hard-working and highly-skilled baker. Draper's delivers to wholesale customers, fresh food shops and retail shops and is renowned for high-quality goods. **Tasks:** serving customers, taking orders, baking to recipe, general food preparation. **Skills:** completetd apprenticeship, hygienic, attention to detail, good people skills, fluent English. Contact: Don Draper d.draper@dbakery...co.uk Tel.: 0044 (0)161 9294696

I/M 2 One of your colleagues does not speak English and asks you to tell him about one of the job ads. Choose one of the ads and give him a brief summary in German. Swap roles.

WORD BANK

family-run company – Familienunternehmen
job application – Bewerbung
opportunities – Möglichkeiten
qualifications – Qualifikationen
skills – Fähigkeiten

Module 5 | Applications

B | Letter of application

R 1 Read the letter of application and decide whether the following statements are true or false. Give reasons for your decisions.

1. Erkan is in the final year of his apprenticeship as a gardener.
2. He has always wanted to be a gardener.
3. Erkan had a holiday job at *Landschaftsgärtnerei Brock*.
4. He is looking forward to working abroad.
5. Erkan has included his CV in the application.

Erkan Celik • Waldstrasse 48 • 50679 Köln • Germany

Michael McCarthy
Vista Landscaping
17 Gorsebrook Rd.
Wolverhampton
WV6 5PI
England

14 October 20_

Dear Mr McCarthy,

Application for job as a gardener

I am writing to apply for the advertised position of a gardener at Vista Landscaping. I completed my apprenticeship as a gardener at a vocational school in Germany six months ago. I have been interested in gardening and plants since I was young and being a gardener is my dream job.
As you will see from my CV, I recently completed a six-month internship at Landschaftsgärtnerei Brock. This not only gave me the opportunity to put my theoretical skills into practice, but I also had the chance to gain more experience with customers.
I am a very enthusiastic person. I am also reliable, responsible and willing to learn. Furthermore, I have good English skills and I would welcome the opportunity to gain some experience working in another country.
Thank you in advance for considering my application. If you require any further information, please contact me.

Yours sincerely,
Erkan Celik

Encl.: CV

M 2 **KMK I** Fassen Sie mit Hilfe der unten stehenden Stichworte die wichtigsten Inhalte des Bewerbungsschreibens auf Deutsch zusammen.

1. Beruf, für den sich Erkan bewirbt   2. Berufserfahrung   3. Motivation
4. Persönliche Qualifikationen/Fähigkeiten   5. Kontaktperson

C | The CV

1 Andrea Wagner ist Auszubildende bei einer IT-Firma in Nürnberg. Sie möchte sich für eine Praktikumsstelle in der englischen Niederlassung ihrer Firma bewerben und fragt David, einen Praktikanten aus England, ob er ihr ein paar Tipps geben kann. Hören Sie das Gespräch an und vervollständigen Sie die folgenden Sätze auf Deutsch.

1. Andrea möchte sich für eine Praktikumsstelle in [?] bewerben.
2. Sie bringt am Montag [?] mit ins Büro.
3. Der Lebenslauf sollte nicht länger sein als [?].
4. Man sollte niemals einen Lebenslauf ohne [?] senden.
5. Man sollte den Lebenslauf dazu benutzen, seine [?] und [?] hervorzuheben.
6. Wenn man seine Arbeitserfahrung auflistet, sollte man mit [?] anfangen.
7. In England muss ein Lebenslauf kein [?] enthalten.
8. Man sollte sicherstellen, dass man zwei [?] nennt.
9. Man sollte niemals [?].
10. Wenn der Lebenslauf fertig ist, sollte man ihn auf [?] und [?] überprüfen.
11. Es ist eine gute Idee, den Lebenslauf [?] zu geben.
12. Wenn man den Lebenslauf abschickt, sollte man [?] behalten.

2 Verfassen Sie ein Anschreiben für eine der in Modulteil A ausgeschriebenen Stellen auf Englisch. Arbeiten Sie dabei die unten aufgeführten Inhalte ein.

→ **PHRASES:** Applications

- Wählen Sie einen geeigneten Betreff.
- Nehmen Sie Bezug auf die Stellenanzeige und bekunden Sie Ihr Interesse an der ausgeschriebenen Stelle.
- Sie werden bald Ihre Ausbildung als … abschließen.
- Bringen Sie zum Ausdruck, dass Sie ein geeigneter Bewerber sind: organisiert, erfahren, hoch motiviert, teamfähig, flexibel, lernbereit, zuverlässig. Sie haben gute Englischkenntnisse.
- Beenden Sie den Brief angemessen und unterschreiben Sie.
- Weisen Sie auf Ihren Lebenslauf hin.

WORD BANK

consider (v) – betrachten
gain (v) – sammeln
internship – Praktikum
letter of application – Bewerbungsschreiben
reliable – zuverlässig
require (v) – benötigen

INFO BOX: Translating German school types and qualifications

It is not always possible to find the equivalent of your school type or qualification in English. However, the following table gives some useful translations.

Schools

Grundschule	Elementary school / Primary school	Berufsschule (Duales System)	Part-time vocational school (dual system)
Hauptschule	General secondary school	Berufsfachschule	Full-time vocational school
Realschule	Intermediate secondary school	Fachschule für technische Berufe	Technical college
Gymnasium	Upper secondary school	Fachoberschule	Upper secondary vocational school
Gesamtschule	Comprehensive school	Fachgymnasium	Specialized upper secondary school

Qualifications

Hauptschulabschluss	secondary modern school qualification	Fachabitur	advanced vocational certificate of education
Mittlere Reife	secondary school leaving certificate	Zusatzqualifikation	additional qualification
Abitur	A level/high school diploma		

Module 6 | Socialising

NACH DIESEM MODUL:

√ kann ich *Small Talk* auf Englisch machen,

√ kenne ich die Regeln des *Small Talk*,

√ kann ich auf Englisch Essen erklären und bestellen.

Socialising

Socialising is very important. It can strengthen relationships with your colleagues and improve the working atmosphere in a company. It can also be a good way of getting to know your customers or potential customers a little better. And in today's global world, English has become the world's language. So although the people you meet and work with are likely to come from a wide range of cultural backgrounds, you will often be required to communicate in English. That means that it is important to not only have the necessary language skills, but also the intercultural knowledge so that you can make a good first impression and develop professional and personal relationships.

I **1** Look at the pictures above. What relationship do you think these people might have to each other? Discuss with your partner.

2 Brainstorm a list of topics these people might be talking about.

P **3** Choose one of the pictures and create a small dialogue.

4 Look at photo 1. Brainstorm what cultural misunderstandings could take place when a German employee meets a person from another country.

P **5** Make a list of situations when a German employee might have contact with foreign colleagues – for example, customers, suppliers, manufacturers, etc.

A | Small talk

Your company has visitors from a subsidiary in Poland. Fabian, a German trainee, has been asked to show Jan, a Polish trainee, around the company.

R 1 Listen to the dialogue between Jan and Fabian. Take notes of the topics the two
⊙ A 1.5 are talking about. Then listen again and make a list of the phrases they use.

2 Name other topics that Jan and Fabian could also talk about.

3 Which of the following topics would / wouldn't you talk about? Why? Discuss in class.

> free-time activities • films you have recently seen • sex • your job or school course • politics • money • personal problems • fashion • sports • food • the boss's wife • the weather • your favourite music • religion

P 4 Small talk is not that difficult. All that is needed is an 'ice breaker' to get things going. Look at the following examples and come up with appropriate answers.

→ **PHRASES:** Socialising

In the workshop:
a. Did you see the game last night?
b. How was your weekend?
c. It's warm today, isn't it?

In the car:
a. How was your trip/flight?
b. Is this your first time in Germany?
c. How's the weather in Sao Paolo?

At a trade fair:
a. Did you have any problems finding our stand?
b. Would you like a brochure?
c. If you like, I could give you a demonstration.

In the canteen:
a. Have you tried the tiramisu? It's amazing!
b. Is anybody sitting here?
c. Ah! I see you like spicy food.

P 5 Now it's your turn to break the ice! Think of at least three ice breakers for each of the following situations:

→ **PHRASES:** Socialising

1. You are at a bar with colleagues on Friday evening.
2. You work with a new colleague one afternoon.
3. You are at the "Green Technology" conference. It's time for a coffee break.
4. You've just arrived at work and you're in the lift. A person you don't know enters.

I 6 Choose one of the four situations above. Start a conversation and try to keep it going for as long as possible. Then end the conversation politely and act it out in front of the class.

→ **PHRASES:** Socialising

P 7 Check the Internet and create your own 'Dos & Don'ts' guide to making small talk and present it to your class. Also include some intercultural aspects.

Dos	Don'ts
Make eye contact.	Ask personal questions.

WORD BANK

subsidiary – Tochtergesellchaft
trainee – Auszubildende(r)

29

B | Small talk in business

R 1 KMK II Ihr Arbeitgeber hat im Internet folgenden Artikel gefunden. Da er nur wenig Englisch kann, bittet er Sie, die folgenden Fragen auf Deutsch zu beantworten.

1. Was wird oft in abwertender Weise über Small Talk gesagt?
2. Was passiert, wenn man sich nicht am Small Talk beteiligt?
3. Was sind die positiven Auswirkungen von Small Talk?

Small talk in business

Small talk is often dismissed as a waste of time, or as the art of saying nothing with a lot of words. Some people say it has no place in the business world, since the subjects discussed are often
5 'unimportant' – i.e. the weather, sports, fashion or other trivial matters. However, if you don't take part in small talk, your business partners might feel that you are being unfriendly or antisocial. When people just stand next to one another,
10 without any signs of communication between them, it can lead to a feeling of uneasiness, and even tension. And this is certainly not good for future business or private relations. Small talk is in fact a very important and effective tool for avoiding an
15 awkward silence between people who don't know each other, especially business partners who may want to form a relationship. Making small talk with strangers helps to break the ice; you discover what they like or dislike, so you can find a common ground of some sort. It helps, for example, if you 20 support the same football team, like the same kind of car, or read the same kinds of books. However, it is also important to know who you are making small talk with. The rules of small talk are not international and different cultures have their own 25 dos and don'ts. For example, you may have been told to always make eye contact when talking to your counterpart – but this may offend a material supplier in China. If you are going to have contact with someone from a different cultural background, 30 it is a good idea to do a little research to avoid any embarassing mistakes.

M 2 KMK II Ihr Arbeitgeber bittet Sie, für die Mitarbeiter stichwortartig ein kurzes Merkblatt anhand dieses Textes auf Deutsch zu erstellen.

R 3 Sind Sie ein guter Smalltalker? Bewerten Sie die Aussagen zum Small Talk in einem Online-Test mit „Yes" oder „No". Notieren Sie die entsprechenden Buchstaben.

Statements	Yes	No
1. Small talk deals with rather unimportant topics. Another word for it is chitchat.	a	c
2. Religion always makes a good topic, because it is controversial.	d	e
3. Answering questions with ‚yes' or ‚no' during small talk is appropriate.	i	e
4. A good answer when asked if you'd like something to drink is: "I'd love a cup of coffee, thank you."	g	h
5. "That's great" is an acceptable answer to the statement: "I got the job!"	b	i
6. The noun "talk" can also mean speech.	a	c
7. Small talk is an icebreaker.	b	f

Addieren Sie die Buchstabenwerte a = 3, b = 3, c = 1, d = 0, e = 0, f = 3, g = 1, h = 1, i = 1.
Wer hat die höchste Zahl? (Maximum 21)

C | Eating out

1 Look at the German words (1.–16.) below and match them with the English equivalent (a.–p.).

1. Speisekarte
2. Rechnung
3. Rind
4. Vorspeise
5. Schweinefleisch
6. Wild
7. durchgebraten
8. Hauptgericht
9. Geflügel
10. Kellner(in)
11. Nachtisch
12. Trinkgeld
13. Beilage
14. vegetarisch
15. herzhaft
16. Gabel

a. well-done
b. pork
c. side order
d. bill
e. game
f. dessert
g. savoury
h. fork
i. menu
j. main dish
k. beef
l. poultry
m. starter
n. waiter/waitress
o. vegetarian
p. tip

2 Partner 1: You are taking a foreign colleague out to dinner in a traditional German restaurant. Study the menu below and explain the dishes to him/her.
Partner 2: Take the role of the foreign colleague and ask questions about the menu.

Gasthaus Sonne

Tagesmenu (10,95 €)

Vorspeisen
Lauchcremesuppe **oder** *kleiner gemischter Salat*

***

Hauptgerichte
Rinderrouladen mit Kartoffelklößen & Sauerkraut
oder
Putenschnitzel mit Pommes Frites
oder
Forelle Müllerin mit Salzkartoffeln

***

Nachtisch
Rote Grütze mit Sahne **oder** *Gemischtes Eis*
(Vanille / Erdbeere / Schoko)

Inklusive ein alkoholfreies Getränk (0,3l)

WORD BANK

avoid (v) – vermeiden
awkward – unangenehm
common ground – gemeinsame Basis
dismiss (v) sth. as – etwas abtun als
tension – Spannung
trivial – unbedeutend
uneasiness – Unbehagen

3 Now the two of you are ready to order. The young German waitress/waiter doesn't mind taking the order in English. Study the eating out phrases at the end of the book and create a role play. Practise, and perform it in front of the class.

→ **PHRASES:** Socialising

Module 7 | Presentations

3b9c4h

7

NACH DIESEM MODUL:

✓ kann ich eine englische Präsentation vorbereiten,

✓ kann ich auf Englisch präsentieren.

Presentations

At some point in your career you may be required to present your company, or their products or services, either informally or on a more formal level. This could mean presenting a new product to a potential customer, or presenting the company as a whole, or something more specific, such as a landscape plan or a suggested menu for an event. Whatever you may be presenting, the ability to give an oral presentation is a key skill. It is also a skill that can be developed and improved.

P 1 Look at the pictures above and describe them using the words below.

> to present • meeting • flipchart • graph • chart • laptop • preparation •
> to explain • sales pitch • audience • projector

P 2 For what reasons might you have to give a presentation? Write a list.

3 With a partner, decide upon a final list and share it with the class.

4 With the same partner brainstorm what you think is important to remember when giving a presentation. Write your answers in a word web like the one below.

A | Preparing a presentation

1 **In the following table are words which are linked to presentations.
Match the English words (1.–10.) with the appropriate German words (a.–j.).**

1. audience	a. Augenkontakt
2. prompt cards	b. beschreiben
3. body language	c. Zusammenfassung
4. eye contact	d. visuelle Hilfsmittel
5. handout	e. Publikum
6. to prepare	f. Schaubild
7. graph	g. Stichwortkarten
8. visual aids	h. Körpersprache
9. to describe	i. vorbereiten
10. summary	j. Informationsblatt

M / KMK II

2 **Fassen Sie den folgenden Text über die Vorbereitung einer Präsentation unter Beantwortung folgender Fragen auf Deutsch zusammen.**

1. Warum soll eine Präsentation nicht schriftlich ausformuliert werden?
2. Wie soll eine Präsentation gegliedert sein?
3. Was ist „signposting"?
4. Welche Vorteile bieten visuelle Hilfsmittel?
5. Wie müssen Präsentationsfolien aussehen, damit sie wirken?

How to make a presentation

You have been asked by your boss to give a presentation? Here are a few tips:
→ Do not write out your presentation in full. Instead, use numbered prompt cards with key words – they are the best way to remember important points.
→ Remember: your presentation needs to have an introduction, a main part, and a conclusion.
→ Begin by giving a brief overview of the points to be covered.
→ Use "signposting" phrases to lead through your presentation, e.g.:

> I would like to begin by … • Let me start by showing you … • Next, I would like to say something about … • Another important point is … • Finally, I will talk about … • In conclusion, …

→ Always finish with a conclusion.

Visual aids
You can use visual aids, such as Powerpoint, to help reinforce what you say.
Visual aids help you explain complicated ideas or technical details more easily and hold the interest of your audience. They also make your presentation look more professional.
If necessary, you can print them out and use them as a handout for the audience.
Visual aids could include graphs, pictures, plans, diagrams, or short texts.
However, if you do use your visual aids to show text, then follow these guidelines:

→ Limit the text to six lines.
→ Try to use no more than six words per line.
→ Print the text in large letters, using upper and lower case letters.
→ Use dark colours, such as black, red, blue, or green. Light colours are difficult to read.

Module 7 | Presentations

3 Match the visual aids (1.–6.) with the pictures below (a.–e.).

1. plan   2. pie chart   3. line graph   4. bar chart   5. diagram   6. table

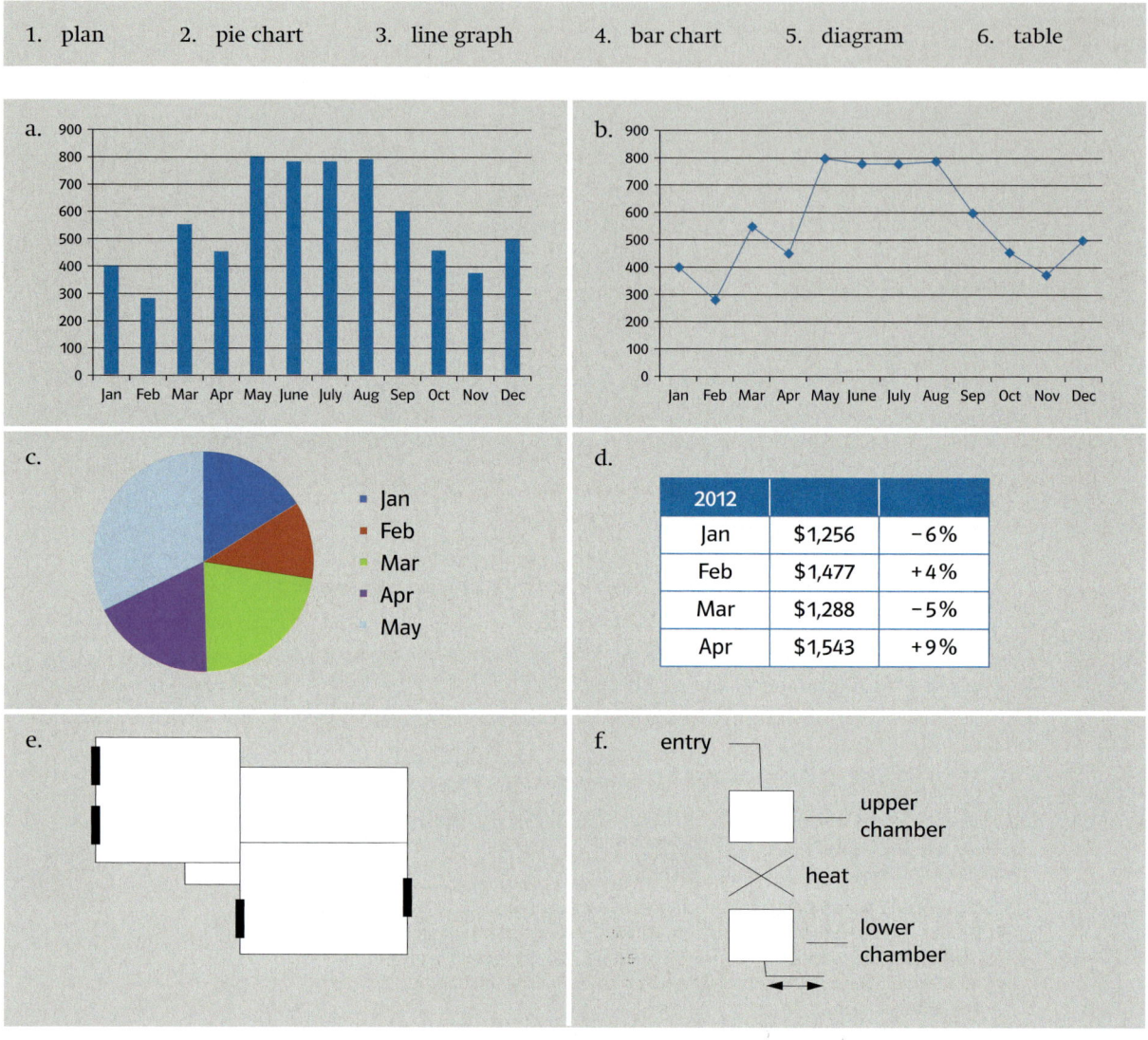

B | Describing materials and products

1 Think of something that you often use and describe it by using the terms in the box to help you. Don't name the item you are describing. Try and write 3 to 5 sentences.

2 Take it in turns to read your sentences to each other and see if you can guess what your partner is describing.

INFO BOX: Useful phrases for describing materials and products
It is a	strong · sturdy · rigid · flexible · lightweight · shiny · robust · matt	material.
The design is	modern · state-of-the-art · classic · elegant · old-fashioned.
It is	user-friendly · difficult to operate · reliable · innovative · hand-crafted.

34

C | Delivering a presentation

R 1 ⊙ A 1.6 Max Wiesinger, a trained carpenter who works for a furniture design company, is presenting a new line of furniture at a trade show. Listen to the presentation and complete the following text.

Good morning ladies and gentleman. Today **1** our new range of **2** , *Simply Wood*. The range, which is shown here on the first slide, includes chairs, a large table, a lounger, and benches. I would like to start by talking about the **3** used in the
5 furniture. All of the *Simply Wood* range is made from single softwood timber and has been **4** by our highly-skilled carpenters and joiners.
If you look at this picture, you can see that the benches and the seats are designed with a low back, deep seats and long arms
10 to offer a great deal of comfort and convenience. Thanks to a special varnish, the furniture is 100 % **5** and will not suffer from discolouring. **6** from this final slide, the furniture is also available in white, to give it a classic, timeless look. And do not worry, we have used a durable white polyurethane coating that is suitable for every environment.
15 On your handout you will see more details about each piece, including the measurements. **7** this morning. Are there any questions? Yes …

P 2 Now it's your turn. Work in small groups and design a chair, a pocket torch, or any other object of your choice. Present your ideas in class. Use the following words and phrases to help you:

→ **PHRASES:** Presentations

> We have designed a … • Our idea was to … • Our design is made of … •
> The advantage of the material we used is … • Its measurements are … •
> length • diameter • weight • width • height • rectangular • circle •
> circular • square • smooth edges • glued/screwed together • made out of one piece

WORD BANK

carpenter – Tischler(in) / Schreiner(in)
circle – Kreis
circular – kreisförmig
diameter – Dicke
furniture – Möbel
height – Höhe
length – Länge
rectangular – rechteckig
smooth – glatt
square – quadratisch
trade show – Messe
weight – Gewicht
width – Breite

M 3 KMK I Ihre Kollegin muss nächste Woche eine wichtige Präsentation halten und bittet Sie um Ihre Hilfe. Sie hat den folgenden Text gefunden, versteht aber leider nur wenig Englisch. Übertragen Sie den Text für sie sinngemäß ins Deutsche.

WORD BANK ⊙

durable – haltbar
joiner – Tischler(in) / Schreiner(in)
polyurethane coating – Polyurethanbeschichtung
softwood – Weichholz
timber – Holz
varnish – Lack

7 Ways to Do it Right: Presentations

1. Keep it short and simple (KISS).
2. Do not use too many visual aids.
3. If you are presenting in a group, decide beforehand who will say what.
4. Practice at least once in front of an audience.
5. Do not read from your notes. Look at your audience.
6. Structure your presentation with phrases so your audience can follow more easily.
7. Tell the audience when they can ask questions – either during the presentation, or at the end.

Module 8 | Dealing with customers 842j42

8

NACH DIESEM MODUL:

✓ kann ich auf Englisch auf Kundenbeschwerden reagieren,

✓ kann ich auf Englisch mit unzufriedenen Kunden umgehen.

Dealing with customers

The way a company deals with its customers is the key to its success. Whether you are arranging appointments, handling enquiries, or dealing with complaints, it is essential that you are able to express yourself clearly, confidently, and politely. And remember: the customer may not always be right, but they are very important.

1 Brainstorm words that describe what is shown in the photos above.

P **2** Compare your list of words with your partner and work together to describe the pictures. Use these words to help you:

> hotline • customer • question • advice • suggestion • chef • butcher • florist • plants • call • unhappy • complain • bill • explain

3 Which of the customers above do you think are happy, and which are unhappy? Explain your answer.

P **4** In what situations do you deal with customers in your job? Copy and complete the word web below to brainstorm reasons for talking to customers.

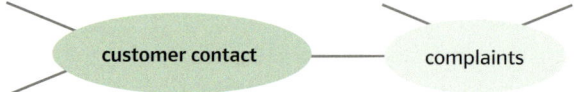

A | Complaints

1 Match the common causes for complaint on the left with the suggested solutions on the right. Several options may be appropriate.

1. delay in delivery	a. offer a price reduction
2. faulty goods	b. improve the service
3. damaged goods	c. repair the goods
4. unsatisfactory services	d. replace the goods
5. wrong goods	e. send the goods by air freight
6. too many/too few goods received	f. send the missing goods
7. too early delivery	g. take the goods back
	h. collect the surplus goods
	i. send a credit note

P **2** What about your industry? Which are the most common reasons for complaints? Make a list and compare it with a partner. Be as specific as possible.

R **3** Which of the following phrases are used for making complaints and which ones for replying to complaints? Make a list.

→ **PHRASES:**
Dealing with customers

1. This is very inconvenient for us because we need the goods urgently.
2. We are sorry for any inconvenience this has caused.
3. We will keep the damaged goods until we hear from you.
4. Please return the damaged goods at our expense.
5. We can assure you that this will not happen again.
6. Some items were badly damaged.
7. We regret to inform you that the order has not yet arrived.
8. We think the damage may have occurred in transit.
9. We are experiencing difficulties with our new logistics software.
10. Could you please look into this problem immediately?
11. Please accept our apologies.
12. The reason for the mistake is that we are extremely busy at this time of the year.
13. Please send us replacements as soon as possible.
14. We hope that this proposal will find your approval.
15. We believe the problem is down to human error.

R **4** You work for *Deutsches Netz*, an IT company in Hamburg. Your boss, Mr Bauder,
KMK II receives a voicemail message on his mobile phone from Mr Jenkins, owner of *New
◉ A 1.7 Wave Marketing*, a subsidiary of an English marketing company based in Hamburg. Listen to the message and answer the following questions.

1. What did the technicians from Deutsches Netz do for New Wave Marketing?
2. What problems are the employees having (three things)?
3. What is the most serious problem?
4. Why is this a serious problem?
5. How should Mr Bauder contact Mr Jenkins?

WORD BANK

hotline – Informationsdienst
technician – Techniker(in)

Module 8 | Dealing with customers

P | 5 Mr Bauder asks you to respond to Mr Jenkins' phone call. He sends you the following email and asks you to draft a short email to the customer.

→ **PHRASES:**
Dealing with customers

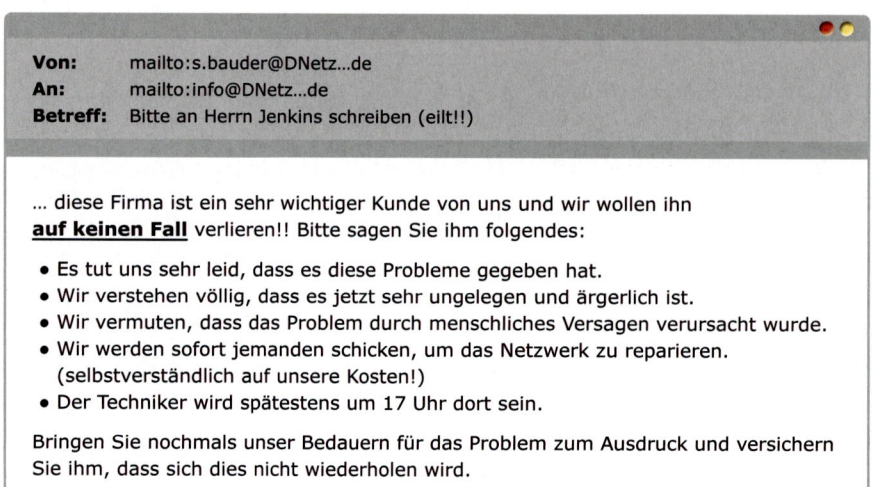

Von: mailto:s.bauder@DNetz...de
An: mailto:info@DNetz...de
Betreff: Bitte an Herrn Jenkins schreiben (eilt!!)

... diese Firma ist ein sehr wichtiger Kunde von uns und wir wollen ihn **auf keinen Fall** verlieren!! Bitte sagen Sie ihm folgendes:

- Es tut uns sehr leid, dass es diese Probleme gegeben hat.
- Wir verstehen völlig, dass es jetzt sehr ungelegen und ärgerlich ist.
- Wir vermuten, dass das Problem durch menschliches Versagen verursacht wurde.
- Wir werden sofort jemanden schicken, um das Netzwerk zu reparieren. (selbstverständlich auf unsere Kosten!)
- Der Techniker wird spätestens um 17 Uhr dort sein.

Bringen Sie nochmals unser Bedauern für das Problem zum Ausdruck und versichern Sie ihm, dass sich dies nicht wiederholen wird.

Danke,
Bauder

M | 6 You work for a plumbing and heating installation company in Leipzig. Your supervisor, Mr Hüber, receives an email about a recent job done for an American family living in the area. Your supervisor does not speak very good English and asks you to read the email and to sum it up in German.

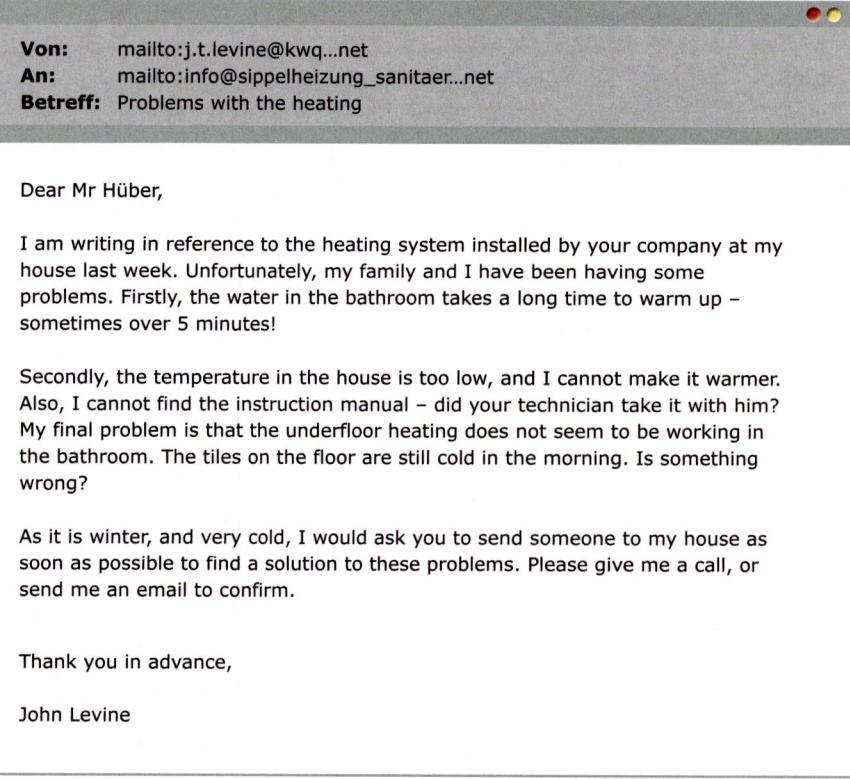

Von: mailto:j.t.levine@kwq...net
An: mailto:info@sippelheizung_sanitaer...net
Betreff: Problems with the heating

Dear Mr Hüber,

I am writing in reference to the heating system installed by your company at my house last week. Unfortunately, my family and I have been having some problems. Firstly, the water in the bathroom takes a long time to warm up – sometimes over 5 minutes!

Secondly, the temperature in the house is too low, and I cannot make it warmer. Also, I cannot find the instruction manual – did your technician take it with him? My final problem is that the underfloor heating does not seem to be working in the bathroom. The tiles on the floor are still cold in the morning. Is something wrong?

As it is winter, and very cold, I would ask you to send someone to my house as soon as possible to find a solution to these problems. Please give me a call, or send me an email to confirm.

Thank you in advance,

John Levine

B | Customer service

P 1 What five tips would you give a colleague about dealing with unhappy customers?

2 Compare your list with a partner.

How to deal with unhappy customers

No company has happy customers 100 % of the time.
Things can always go wrong and customers can become unhappy – or worse, upset. Here are some tips on how to avoid making the situation worse.

Stay calm: The customer may be angry at somebody, but it does not help the situation if you get just as angry. The last thing you want to do is start an argument – that is very unprofessional and unhelpful. Try to calm the customer down.

Listen, listen, listen: You will only be able to understand what has upset the customer if you listen, and listen carefully. Before you start talking, listen actively to the customer until you fully understand why they are unhappy. If you don't know what's wrong, you will not be able to do anything about it.

The customer is king: Show the customer that they, and their problem, are important to you. Tell them quickly how sorry you are for their problem and reassure them that you will do everything you can to help them. And, always be patient and polite.

Stay positive: Do your best to stay positive at all times. Remember that your goal is to solve the problem and you can do this better if you have a positive frame of mind. Regardless of how negative and furious the customer gets, it is important that you do not let it affect your mood.

No excuses: No matter what the problem is, or who you think caused it, do not blame other people or try to make excuses. Instead, take the initiative and do whatever you can to solve the problem.

R 3 Find the synonyms in the text for the following words and expressions:

1. to stop sth. from happening
2. disagreement
3. to aim
4. to fix
5. attitude
6. very angry
7. reason
8. to take control

R 4 Sie lesen den oben stehenden Artikel im Internet. Beantworten Sie die folgenden
KMK II Fragen dazu in ganzen Sätzen auf Deutsch.

1. Warum ist es wichtig zu wissen, wie man mit unzufriedenen Kunden umgeht?
2. Was sollte man tun, wenn der Kunde sehr verärgert ist?
3. Warum ist es wichtig, dem Kunden ganz genau zuzuhören?
4. Wie kann man einem Kunden zeigen, dass man sein Problem ernst nimmt?
5. Wann ist es gerechtfertigt, jemand anderem die Schuld für das vorliegende Problem zu geben?

I 5 Choose one of the problems you listed in exercise A1 and create a short role play. One of you should play the unhappy / angry customer and the other the employee. Act out your role play in front of the class.

WORD BANK

instruction manual – Bedienungsanleitung
plumbing and heating – Heizung und Sanitär
underfloor heating – Fußbodenheizung

V1 Company tour

Before watching
1. Describe the photo.
2. Who do you think the men in the picture are?

While watching
3. Watch the film and find out the following:
   a. the number of countries SAND Machinery delivers to.
   b. the names of three departments that the men have visited.
   c. the number of people who work for the company.
   d. whether SAND Machinery has other sites and if so, where they are.
4. Watch the film again and answer the questions.
   a. What will Mr Kramer's main tasks be during the internship?
   b. What is made at the company's production site?

After watching
5. Explain the sentences from the clip in your own words.
   a. "I'm eager to get in and get my feet wet."
   b. "… around the globe, around the clock."

V2 Telephoning

Before watching
1. Describe the photo.

While watching
2. What problem does Ralf have at the beginning of the call?
3. Watch the film again and answer the questions.
   a. Who is calling?
   b. Who does he want to speak to?
   c. What is the purpose of his call?
   d. Why can Ralf's boss not contact the caller until the 15th of the month?
4. Find out the following technical information about the vehicle in question:
   a. the engine size
   b. the top speed
   c. the distance that can be travelled on a single charge.

After watching
5. Use the information in parts 3 and 4 to write a short memo for Ralf's boss explaining who called and what the call was about, and giving other key information.
6. How does Ralf handle the phone call? Discuss what he did well and what he could improve.

ⓕ V3 Job interview

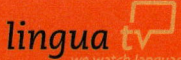

Before watching
1. Describe the photo.

While watching
2. Write down three of the questions that the interviewer asks.
3. Watch the film again and answer the questions.
   a. What is the applicant's name?
   b. What position is he applying for?
   c. What position did the applicant hold in his last job?
   d. According to the applicant, what is his greatest strength?
   e. What is the applicant's weakness?
   f. What questions does the applicant ask the interviewer?

After watching
4. Do you think the applicant will get the job? Give reasons for your answer.

ⓕ V4 Technical support

While watching
1. What does 'rebooting the system' mean?
2. Watch the video again and decide whether the following statements are true or false.
   a. The caller cannot connect to the Internet.
   b. He has been having problems for two days now.
   c. He has tried rebooting the system.
   d. Turning the modem on and off did not help the problem.
   e. The scanner is not connected to the caller's computer.
   f. The technical support employee is unable to solve the problem with the scanner.

After watching
3. Make a list of problems that employees may have with their computers.
4. Record the call by copying the headings onto a sheet of paper and filling in the information.

   Name of caller · Problem(s) · Solution(s) · Further action necessary: Yes/No

Video lounge |

📹 V 5 Waste – the future's most valuable resource ZDF.enterprises

Before watching
1. What things do you recycle every day, and how?
2. How many different waste bins does your city or community provide per household?

While watching
3. Watch the film and find out the following information:
   a. How many tons of rubbish does Germany produce each year?
   b. What nations are eager to pay for our rubbish?
   c. What metal is particularly desirable for recycling?

4. Watch the film again and answer the following questions:
   a. How many tons of copper were stolen in Germany?
   b. How much heat can one ton of residual waste produce?

After watching
5. Explain these phrases/sentences from the film in your own words.
   a. "modern urban warfare"
   b. "Our waste is getting a second lease on life."

📹 V 6 Pipe inspection ZDF.enterprises

Before watching
1. What do pipelines transport?

While watching
2. Watch the film and find out the following information:
   a. What is the inspection device called?
   b. How long is it?
   c. How fast does the device travel?
   d. How many days does it take to inspect 300 km of pipeline?

3. Watch the film again and answer the following questions:
   a. Where are the data analyzed?
   b. How accurate is the data grid?
   c. What does the device use to identify defects?

After watching
4. What may cause defects in or damage to pipelines?

V 7 High voltage work

Before watching
1. What do you think the men in the steel basket are preparing to do?

While watching
2. Watch the film and find out the following:
   a. what weather conditions are necessary for repairing overhead power lines.
   b. how many volts of electricity high-voltage lines carry.
   c. how the repairmen get to the damaged lines.
   d. what safety measures are taken.

3. Watch the film again and answer the following questions:
   a. How long does the job shown in the film take?
   b. Where is the electricity switched off and on?

After watching
4. Why is it important that the men work quickly?
5. Explain in your own words: "A power cut can quickly bring an entire city to its knees."

V 8 Ras Laffan

While watching
1. Watch the film and find out the following:
   a. where Ras Laffan is located.
   b. what is processed there.
   c. how much is processed each year.
   d. how large the Ras Laffan industrial region is.

2. Watch the film again and answer the following:
   a. What problems do the construction workers face?
   b. How is the concrete cooled, and why?
   c. Why is the gas cooled?

After watching
3. Explain the phrase "liquid gold".

Video lounge

V 9 Pipelines

Before watching
1. Name some things which are transported in pipelines.

While watching
2. Watch the film and find out the following:
   a. what alloy is popular for making long-distance pipelines.
   b. how thick are the steel plates that are formed into round pipes.
   c. the welding technique used in the factory shown.
   d. what the expander is for.

3. Watch the film again and answer the following:
   a. What conditions do offshore pipelines have to cope with?
   b. Why do they have an additional outer casing of concrete?

After watching
4. Explain why quality-control checks are important in the production of pipelines.

V 10 Robots in the hospital

While watching
1. Watch the film and find out the following:
   a. What hospital is shown as an example? Which parts of the hospital do we see?
   b. How many robots do they have?
   c. What powers the robot couriers and how do they navigate?
   d. What is a 'lift-and-tunnel system'?

2. Watch the film again and answer these questions:
   a. What metal in the plates keeps the food warm?
   b. Do the robots distribute the food to the patients?
   c. How many containers are used to transport food?
   d. How does the hospital director feel about using robots to transport patients?

After watching
3. What else do you think the robots transport in the hospital?
4. Where else might transportation robots be used?

V11 Portable power stations

BBC Motion Gallery

Before watching
1. Think of situations in which a portable power station like the one in the photo could be useful.

While watching
2. Watch the film and list the uses of electrical power 'out in the open' that the reporter mentions.

3. Watch the film again and answer the following:
   a. What supplies the power for the 12-volt portable power station?
   b. Why are batteries not such a good choice?
   c. Where was the portable power station invented?

After watching
4. Do you think the inventor will be able to sell his power station in Germany? Where might the need for it be greater?

V12 Car speed control

BBC Motion Gallery

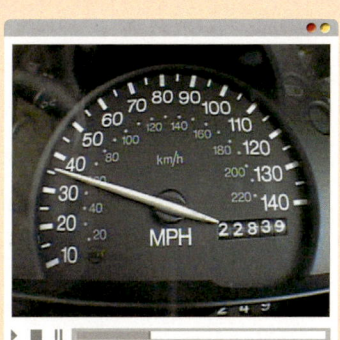

Before watching
1. What speed limit is acceptable
   a. on city streets?
   b. on the motorway?

While watching
2. Watch the film and find out the following:
   a. how many people die in road accidents in the UK every year.
   b. what the MIRA is working on.
   c. what the satellite positioning system does.

3. Watch the film again and answer the following:
   a. Is speed control popular with car manufacturers? Why or why not?
   b. Do speed cameras have any effect on driving habits?
   c. How is the speed-control system being tested?

After watching
4. Would you buy a car with a speed-control system? Give reasons for your answer.

KMK-Prüfungssatz

KMK Stufe I *(100 VP)*

1 Rezeption (Hörverstehen) — 20 VP

A 6.1 Sie interessieren sich für eine Stelle im englischsprachigen Ausland, z. B. ein Praktikum oder eine längerfristige Anstellung nach der Gesellen- oder Facharbeiterprüfung. Die Virtual Employment Agency (VEA) vermittelt solche Praktika. Sie laden einen Podcast mit vier Stellenangeboten herunter. Erstellen Sie hierzu eine Tabelle mit folgenden Stichwörtern und hören Sie den Podcast zweimal an. Füllen Sie Ihre Tabelle auf Englisch aus.

Information number	1 *(5 VP)*	2 *(5 VP)*	3 *(5 VP)*	4 *(5 VP)*
trade/position offered				
length of practical				
company and location of practical				
requirements				
extra information: email address, telephone number if given				

2 Rezeption (Leseverstehen) — 20 VP

Sie möchten Ihren Arbeitgeber überzeugen, Sie während Ihrer Ausbildung für ein Praktikum im Ausland freizustellen und haben dazu folgendes Informationsmaterial von der Internetseite der VEA heruntergeladen. Ihr Arbeitgeber bittet Sie, folgende Fragen zu diesem Text auf Deutsch zu beantworten.

1. Was erfahren wir über die Organisation der VEA? *(2 VP)*
2. Welche Vorteile eines Praktikums werden genannt? *(3 VP)*
3. Was konkret bietet die VEA an? *(3 VP)*
4. Was wird über eine Bezahlung/Kostenzuschuss für die Praktikanten gesagt? *(3 VP)*
5. Wie lange dauern die angebotenen Praktika? *(3 VP)*
6. Wer kann sich bei der VEA bewerben und welche Voraussetzungen sollten die Bewerber mitbringen? *(3 VP)*
7. Wie bewirbt man sich? Welche Unterlagen müssen geschickt werden? *(3 VP)*

> **London-based VEA offers job placements**
>
> *Who we are*
> VEA is an organisation funded by the European Union and European companies. Our aim is to help to make European companies fit to
> 5 operate more effectively in a global world by giving their trainees a chance to work abroad, improve their English language skills and become acquainted with a new culture. The trainees who take part in the programme have a chance to see different work techniques and learn to adapt to new working conditions.

What we offer

VEA helps trainees to find work placements in England, Scotland and
Wales. We have lists of companies in all kinds of trades who offer
work placements. All placements take place in an authentic work
environment. We can help you to establish contacts with companies
and to plan your stay. We have a telephone hotline if problems should
come up.

What payment is given

VEA does not pay trainees any money for the work placement, but we
can pay a fixed amount towards your travelling expenses. However,
most of the companies that we have under contract offer small salaries
that will enable you to cover daily expenses such as food and board.

How long do work placements last?

The duration of work placements depends on the companies.
Placements usually last between eight and ten weeks, but most
companies are flexible if you want to arrange different periods. The
shortest possible placement is three weeks.

Who can apply

All trainees can apply after their first or second year of training. The
applicants should have a fair working knowledge of English. They
should be communicative, interested in our culture and willing to
participate in social activities if these are offered by the company.

How to apply

Send an email and a CV as an attachment in English telling us why
you would like to take part in our work placement programme. You
should also send written consent and a letter of recommendation from
your company. And don't forget to mention the dates you would like to
do the placement and the trade you would like to work in. Send your
application by email to info@vea…biz subject matter "work placement."

(363 words)

---

3 Produktion — 30 VP

Sie wollen sich per E-Mail bei der VEA um ein Praktikum bewerben (Adresse: info@vea…biz). Schreiben Sie, dass Ihre Firma es lieber hätte, wenn Sie zunächst einmal nur 3 Wochen auf ein Auslandspraktikum gingen. Geben Sie an, welchen Beruf Sie lernen und in welchem Jahr Ihrer Ausbildung Sie sich befinden. Nennen Sie einen Zeitraum von drei Wochen (mit genauem Datum), in dem Sie ein Praktikum machen möchten.

4 Mediation — 30 VP

Auf der Internetseite befinden sich auch Erfahrungsberichte früherer Absolventen. Einer hat Ihnen besonders gefallen. Sie übertragen ihn ins Deutsche, um ihn ebenfalls Ihrem Arbeitgeber vorzulegen. Auf eine wörtliche Übersetzung legt er keinen Wert, lediglich auf eine inhaltlich korrekte Wiedergabe.

> My name is Michael. I'm in my third year of training as a car mechanic. I've just come back from a three-month placement in South Wales. It was sponsored by the Leonardo Programme. My company in Germany ▶

encouraged me to apply for the placement. They even sponsored me by paying my wages even though I wasn't working for them for three months.

I worked in a company based near Cardiff that makes parts for the automobile industry. First I spent a few days in each department of the company, and then I was fully involved in the production process.

I worked with a Welsh colleague in the CNC centre. Of course I had some experience with CNC from my own company. I must say, I learned a lot, especially how to work more efficiently and independently.

In the beginning the language was a bit of a problem, but after a couple of weeks we managed to communicate quite well, and I learned many technical words and phrases.

This placement was a great opportunity for me, and my boss sees it as a real plus for our company and our business with British customers.

(193 words)

Role cards

Modul 3 Telephoning, B 3

Speaker A

Give your partner the following information:
1. The room is 54 m².
2. The wire needs to be 128.5 cm long.
3. The doors are 80 cm x 220 cm.
4. Each of the components weighs around 0.75 kg.

Modul 3 Telephoning, B 3

Speaker B

Give your partner the following information:
1. The table is 2 m x 3 m.
2. The engine runs at 7500 rpm.
3. 220 V sockets are standard in Germany.
4. The customer would like the work surface to be 24 mm thick.

Phrases

1 | Meeting people

Formal greetings	Formelle Begrüßung
Good morning / afternoon / evening, Ms Robinson / Mr Jones.	Guten Morgen / Tag / Abend, Frau Robinson / Herr Jones.
Good morning / afternoon / evening, ladies and gentlemen.	Guten Morgen / Tag / Abend, meine Damen und Herren.
Informal greetings	**Informelle Begrüßung**
Good morning, Susan / James.	Guten Morgen, Susan / James.
Hi / Hello / Morning, Karl.	Tag / Morgen, Karl.
Hi everybody!	Tag zusammen!
Formal goodbyes	**Formelle Verabschiedung**
Goodbye! It's been nice / pleasant meeting you.	Auf Wiedersehen! Es war nett / angenehm, Sie kennen zu lernen!
Thank you for your help / your time. Let's keep in touch.	Danke für Ihre Hilfe / Ihre Zeit. Wir bleiben in Kontakt.
Informal goodbyes	**Informelle Verabschiedung**
Bye!	Tschüss / Ciao!
See you later!	Bis später!
See you around!	Wir sehen uns!
See you tomorrow / on Monday / next week!	Bis morgen / Montag / nächste Woche!
Formal introduction	**Formelle Vorstellung**
May I introduce myself?	Darf ich mich vorstellen?
Hello, my name is / I'm Lukas Hansen from ATW Shipping.	Hallo, mein Name ist / ich heiße Lukas Hansen von ATW Shipping.
Pleased to meet you. / Nice to meet you. / How do you do?	Angenehm. / Sehr erfreut.
It's a pleasure to finally meet you in person.	Es freut mich sehr, Sie endlich einmal persönlich kennen zu lernen.
Informal introduction	**Informelle Vorstellung**
Hi. I'm Peter, Peter James.	Hi. Ich bin Peter, Peter James.
Hello, my name is Sarah O'Neill.	Hallo, ich heiße Sarah O'Neill.
Hi Sarah. Nice to meet you.	Hi Sarah. Freut mich, dich kennen zu lernen.

Introducing others (formal)	Andere miteinander bekannt machen (formell)
Have you met our managing director?	Haben Sie schon unsere Geschäftsführerin / unseren Geschäftsführer kennen gelernt?
Ms Hall? May I introduce you to Christian Eriksen, our new intern? Christian, Georgina Hall from our sales department.	Frau Hall? Darf ich Sie Christian Eriksen, unserem neuen Praktikanten, vorstellen? Christian, das ist Georgina Hall von unserer Verkaufsabteilung.
Introducing others (informal)	**Andere miteinander bekannt machen (informell)**
Here's someone I'd like you to meet.	Ich möchte euch gerne jemanden vorstellen.
Christian, this is Joe. Joe, Christian.	Christian, das ist Joe. Joe, das ist Christian.
Let me introduce you to the team.	Darf ich dich dem Team vorstellen?
Use of first names	**Verwendung von Vornamen**
Please call me Martin.	Bitte nennen Sie mich ruhig Martin.
My name's Marianne.	Ich heiße Marianne.
My first name's Andrew, but everybody calls me Andy.	Mein Vorname ist Andrew, aber alle nennen mich Andy.
May I call you Anna?	Darf ich Anna zu Ihnen sagen?

2 | Your company

Introducing the company	Die Firma vorstellen
Our company was founded in 1997.	Unsere Firma wurde 1997 gegründet.
In 2005 we were taken over by …	2005 wurden wir von … übernommen.
We are a leading manufacturer of engines.	Wir sind ein führender Hersteller von Motoren.
We are a medium-sized family firm.	Wir sind ein mittelständisches Familienunternehmen.
We are a manufacturer of industrial cleaning machines specializing in high-pressure cleaners.	Wir sind ein Hersteller von industriellen Reinigungsgeräten und sind auf Hochdruckreiniger spezialisiert.
I work for a major construction company.	Ich arbeite bei einem bedeutenden Bauunternehmen.
We are a subsidiary of …	Wir sind eine Tochtergesellschaft von …
We are a chain of electronics suppliers.	Wir sind eine Kette von Elektronik-Anbietern.
Describing the company's products / services	**Die Produkte / Dienstleistungen der Firma beschreiben**
We offer sustainable solutions.	Wir bieten nachhaltige Lösungen an.
Our products are environmentally friendly.	Unsere Produkte sind umweltfreundlich.
Our products are well-known in Europe.	Unsere Produkte sind europaweit bekannt.
Our components are both reliable and long-lasting.	Unsere Komponenten sind zuverlässig und haben eine lange Lebensdauer.
Our software is adapted to suit your requirements.	Unsere Software wird Ihren Bedürfnissen angepasst.
We manufacture high-tech shock absorbers.	Wir stellen High-Tech-Stoßdämpfer her.
Our products are designed using the latest CAD technology.	Unsere Produkte werden mit der neuesten CAD-Technologie entworfen.

Appendix | Phrases

Describing the job	Den Beruf beschreiben
I'm training to become a …	Ich mache eine Lehre / Ausbildung zur / zum …
I am a bricklayer / carpenter / technician / plumber / joiner.	Ich bin Maurer(in), Zimmermann / Zimmerin, Techniker(in), Klempner(in), Schreiner(in).
I work in the automotive industry.	Ich arbeite in der Automobilindustrie.
I work with automated machines.	Ich arbeite mit automatisierten Maschinen.
Describing the workplace	**Den Arbeitsplatz beschreiben**
I work on an assembly line / a machine.	Ich arbeite am Fließband / an einer Maschine.
I work in a large warehouse / factory.	Ich arbeite in einem großen Warenlager / einer großen Fabrik.
I work in a garage / workshop.	Ich arbeite in einer Autowerkstatt / Werkstatt.
I work on a building site.	Ich arbeite auf einer Baustelle.
Talking about tasks and responsibilities	**Über Aufgaben und Zuständigkeiten sprechen**
I am responsible for programming the machines.	Ich bin für die Programmierung der Maschinen zuständig.
I report to the foreman.	Ich bin dem Meister / Vorarbeiter unterstellt.
I work shifts.	Ich mache Schichtarbeit.
I often have to do overtime.	Ich muss oft Überstunden machen.
I repair electrical devices.	Ich repariere elektrische Geräte.

3 | Telephoning

1. Answering the phone	Sich am Telefon melden
Introducing yourself	**Sich vorstellen**
Smart EDV GmbH, good morning. Hendrik Klopp speaking.	Smart EDV GmbH, guten Morgen. Hendrik Klopp am Apparat.
Offering help	**Hilfe anbieten**
How may I help you? / Can I help you?	(Wie) kann ich Ihnen helfen?
What can I do for you?	Was kann ich für Sie tun?
Asking for details	**Nach Details fragen**
Who's calling, please?	Wer ist am Apparat, bitte?
May I / Can I ask who's calling, please?	Darf ich fragen, wer anruft?
May I / can I take your name, please?	Könnten Sie mir bitte Ihren Namen nennen?
Could you spell that please?	Könnten Sie das bitte buchstabieren?

Connecting	Verbinden
One moment, please. I'm putting you through now.	Einen Moment bitte, ich verbinde Sie.
Shall I put you through to …?	Soll ich Sie mit … verbinden?
Hold the line, please. I'll put you through.	Bitte bleiben Sie am Apparat. Ich verbinde.
Your boss is not available	**Der / die Vorgesetzte ist nicht zu sprechen**
I'm afraid Mr Deschler is not in the office at the moment.	Es tut mir leid, Herr Deschler ist z. Zt. leider nicht in seinem Büro.
… He is on a building site.	… Er ist auf einer Baustelle.
… He has a visitor with him.	… Er hat Besuch.
… He is out at lunch.	… Er ist in der Mittagspause.
Offering to call back	**Einen Rückruf anbieten**
Shall I ask her to call you back?	Soll ich sie bitten, Sie zurückzurufen?
Can she call you back this afternoon?	Kann sie Sie heute Nachmittag zurückrufen?
Does he have your telephone number?	Hat er Ihre Telefonnummer?
Can I just confirm your number?	Kann ich Ihre Nummer nochmals überprüfen?
I'll just repeat that.	Ich wiederhole.
Taking a message	**Eine Nachricht aufnehmen**
Can I take a message?	Kann ich etwas ausrichten?
Can I give him a message?	Kann ich ihm etwas ausrichten?
Would you like to leave a message?	Möchten Sie eine Nachricht hinterlassen?
Can I just confirm that?	Kann ich das kurz überprüfen?
So that's twenty-four square metres, isn't it?	Das sind also vierundzwanzig Quadratmeter, oder?
I'll make sure he gets the message.	Ich werde mich darum kümmern, dass er die Nachricht bekommt.
I'll tell her as soon as she comes back.	Ich sage ihr Bescheid, sobald sie zurückkommt.
Problems	**Probleme**
Sorry, I didn't quite catch that. Could you repeat it more slowly, please?	Es tut mir leid, das habe ich nicht verstanden. Könnten Sie es bitte etwas langsamer wiederholen?
I'm afraid I didn't catch the telephone number. Could you repeat it, please?	Leider habe ich die Telefonnummer nicht mitbekommen. Würden Sie sie bitte wiederholen?
I'm sorry, but we are having a bad connection. Could you repeat that, please?	Es tut mir leid, aber die Verbindung ist schlecht. Könnten Sie das bitte nochmals wiederholen?
Ending the call	**Das Telefongespräch beenden**
You're welcome.	Bitteschön. / Gern geschehen.
Thanks for calling.	Vielen Dank für Ihren Anruf.
Goodbye.	Auf Wiederhören.

2. Making a call	Jemanden anrufen
Introducing yourself	**Sich vorstellen**
This is … from Fertighaus Henke.	Hier spricht … von Fertighaus Henke.
My name's … I'm calling from Smart EDV.	Mein Name ist … . Ich rufe von der Firma Smart EDV an.
Asking to speak to somebody	**Nach jemandem fragen**
Could I speak to Ms Sheringham, please?	Könnte ich bitte Frau Sheringham sprechen?
Could you put me through to Mr Ferguson?	Könnten Sie mich mit Herrn Ferguson verbinden?
Could you give me his / her extension number, please?	Könnten Sie mir bitte seine / ihre Durchwahl geben?
I'd like to speak to someone from the production planning department.	Ich möchte mit jemandem in der Fertigungsplanung sprechen.
Spelling your name	**Den Namen buchstabieren**
It's S-C-H-N-E-I-D-E-R. Schneider.	Das ist S-C-H-N-E-I-D-E-R. Schneider.
Giving your phone number	**Die Telefonnummer nennen**
It's 0049 for Germany, then 0391 458 547.	Das ist die 0049 für Deutschland, dann 0391 458 547.
It's 0391 458 547.	Das ist die 0391 458 547.
Leaving a message	**Eine Nachricht hinterlassen**
Yes, please. Could you tell him that …?	Ja bitte. Könnten Sie ihm ausrichten, dass …?
Thank you. I'll ring back later.	Danke sehr. Ich rufe später zurück.
I'm afraid I won't be in the workshop this afternoon. I'll give you my mobile number.	Leider bin ich heute Nachmittag nicht in der Werkstatt. Ich gebe Ihnen meine Handynummer.
Ending the call	**Das Telefongespräch beenden**
Thank you very much for your help.	Vielen Dank für Ihre Hilfe.
Goodbye.	Auf Wiederhören.

4 | Written communication

Salutation	Anrede
Dear Sir or Madam	Sehr geehrte Damen und Herren
Dear Mr … / Dear Ms …	Lieber Herr … / Liebe Frau …
Dear Peter	Lieber Peter
Complimentary close	**Schlussformel**
Yours sincerely / Yours faithfully (rarely used)	Mit freundlichen Grüßen / Hochachtungsvoll (selten benutzt)
Best regards / Kind regards / Best wishes	Schöne Grüße / Herzliche Grüße

Enquiries	Anfragen
We have visited your website and …	Wir haben Ihre Webseite besucht und …
Your services have been recommended to us by …	Ihre Dienstleistungen wurden uns von … empfohlen.
We are a well-established manufacturer of …	Wir sind ein gut etablierter Hersteller von …
Our firm is a leading importer of …	Unsere Firma ist ein führender Importeur von …
Could you please let us have a brochure and a price list?	Wir bitten um einen Prospekt und eine Preisliste.
Please send us a quotation for …	Bitte machen Sie uns ein Angebot über …
Please quote your lowest prices for …	Bitte nennen Sie uns Ihre günstigsten Preise für …
We would be grateful for information on your terms of payment and delivery.	Wir bitten um nähere Angaben zu Ihren Liefer- und Zahlungsbedingungen.
A visit by your representative would be appreciated.	Wir wären dankbar für einen Besuch Ihres Vertreters.
We look forward to hearing from you.	Wir freuen uns darauf, bald von Ihnen zu hören.
Offers	**Angebote**
Many thanks for your enquiry of 30 May about our new range of …	Wir danken Ihnen vielmals für Ihre Anfrage vom 30. Mai wegen unseres neuen Sortiments von …
As requested, we are sending you enclosed our latest catalogue and price list.	Wie gewünscht fügen wir unseren neuesten Katalog und unsere Preisliste bei.
We can offer a 10 % quantity discount on orders of at least 500 units.	Für Aufträge über mindestens 500 Stück wird 10 % Mengenrabatt gewährt.
We take pleasure in submitting the following cost estimate:	Wir freuen uns, Ihnen folgenden Kostenvoranschlag zu unterbreiten:
Our usual terms of payment are: – cash with order – cash on delivery – 30 days net, 10 days 2 % – by irrevocable letter of credit	Unsere üblichen Zahlungsbedingungen lauten: – Barzahlung bei Auftragserteilung – Barzahlung bei Lieferung – 30 Tage netto, 10 Tage 2 % Skonto – durch unwiderrufliches und bestätigtes Akkreditiv
The delivery period is 6 weeks.	Die Lieferzeit beträgt 6 Wochen.
We look forward to welcoming you as our customers.	Wir freuen uns darauf, Sie als Kunden begrüßen zu dürfen.
Orders	**Bestellungen**
Please supply the following items on the terms stated below:	Bitte liefern Sie uns folgende Positionen zu den unten genannten Bedingungen:
As agreed, we will effect payment by bank transfer 30 days from date of invoice.	Wie vereinbart werden wir die Zahlung 30 Tage nach Rechnungsdatum per Banküberweisung vornehmen lassen.
Please note that the goods must reach us by 1 March at the latest.	Wir weisen darauf hin, dass die Ware bis spätestens 1. März hier eintreffen muss.
Please acknowledge this order promptly.	Bitte bestätigen Sie diesen Auftrag umgehend.
We look forward to receiving the goods in time and to doing further business with you.	Wir freuen uns, die Ware rechtzeitig entgegennehmen und weitere Geschäfte mit Ihnen machen zu können.

5 | Applications

Mentioning the source of the advertisement	Die Quelle der Anzeige nennen
I would like to apply for the job / work placement which you advertised in the … of … / on the … website.	Ich möchte mich auf die in der … vom … / auf der … Website ausgeschriebenen Stelle / Praktikumsstelle bewerben.
I saw your advertisement for a … (job / work placement) in the … of … / on the … website and would like to apply for the position.	Ich habe Ihre Anzeige für eine Stelle / Praktikumsstelle in der … vom … / auf der … Website gesehen und möchte mich auf die Stelle bewerben.
I am writing in response to your advertisement of … in the … / on the … website for a … (job / work placement).	Ich melde mich auf Ihre Anzeige vom … in der … / auf der … Website für eine Stelle / Praktikumsstelle.
Introducing yourself	**Sich vorstellen**
I am particularly attracted to this position as …	Ich bin an dieser Stelle besonders interessiert, weil …
I am currently doing a one-year / two-year … apprenticeship at a vocational college in … (town), Germany.	Ich mache zurzeit eine ein-/zweijährige … Ausbildung an einer berufsbildenden Schule in …, Deutschland.
I am in the second year of an apprenticeship in …	Ich bin im zweiten Jahr einer Ausbildung als …
At present I am working as a … with … (company).	Zurzeit arbeite ich als … bei der Firma …
After completing my apprenticeship / At the end of the apprenticeship I will be a qualified (job title).	Nachdem ich meine Ausbildung beendet habe / Mit Abschluss meiner Ausbildung bin ich eine qualifizierte / ein qualifizierter (Berufsbezeichnung).
Talking about yourself and saying why you are a good applicant	**Über sich sprechen und begründen, warum man ein guter Bewerber / eine gute Bewerberin ist**
As you will see from my CV …	Wie aus meinem Lebenslauf zu ersehen ist, …
I have a good knowledge of …	Ich verfüge über gute Kenntnisse in …
I am motivated / reliable / hard-working / keen to learn / friendly / open / a good communicator.	Ich bin motiviert / zuverlässig / sehr fleißig / lernwillig / freundlich / aufgeschlossen / ein kommunikativer Mensch.
I have previous work experience as …	Ich verfüge bereits über Berufserfahrung als …
I have a wide range of interests including …	Ich bin vielseitig interessiert, u.a. an …
I am familiar with this kind of work, because …	Mit dieser Tätigkeit bin ich vertraut, da …
I would very much welcome the opportunity to work in …	Über die Möglichkeit, in … zu arbeiten, würde ich mich sehr freuen.
I believe that I would be a valuable / enthusiastic employee.	Ich bin überzeugt, dass ich ein(e) nützliche(r) / engagierte(r) Mitarbeiter(in) wäre.

Finishing the letter	Den Brief beenden
I hope that you will consider my application.	Ich hoffe, dass Sie meine Bewerbung in Betracht ziehen werden.
Thank you in advance for considering my application.	Ich danke Ihnen im Voraus, dass Sie meine Bewerbung in Betracht ziehen.
I look forward to hearing from you (soon).	Ich freue mich auf eine (baldige) Antwort.

6 | Socialising

Ice breakers	Eisbrecher
How was your weekend? – Good, thanks. How about yours?	Wie war dein / Ihr Wochenende? – Gut, danke. Und bei dir / Ihnen?
Did you see the game last night? – Of course! It was unbelievable. What did you think about the red card / winning goal?	Hast du / Haben Sie das Spiel gestern abend gesehen? – Natürlich! Es war unglaublich. Was halten Sie von der roten Karte / vom Siegtor?
Quite cold / warm today, isn't it?	Ziemlich kalt / warm heute, oder?
I really like your watch. Where did you get it?	Ihre / deine Uhr gefällt mir wirklich gut. Woher haben Sie / hast du sie?
Did you read the story about … in the newspaper this morning?	Haben Sie heute Morgen den Bericht über … in der Zeitung gelesen?
Ah! I see you are also in need of a coffee / cup of tea.	Ah! Wie ich sehe brauchen Sie / brauchst du auch einen Kaffee / eine Tasse Tee.
Is this your first time in Germany?	Sind Sie / Bist du zum ersten Mal in Deutschland?
The food is pretty good here, isn't it? – You can say that again!	Das Essen hier ist ziemlich gut, oder? – Das können Sie / kannst du laut sagen.
Keeping the conversation going	**Das Gespräch in Gang halten**
Really? Is that right? You're joking!	Wirklich? Ist das wahr? Sie machen / du machst Scherze!
That's brilliant / hilarious / fascinating!	Das ist brilliant / sehr lustig / faszinierend!
And what happened then?	Und was passierte dann?
No, unfortunately I missed it. What happened?	Nein, leider habe ich es verpasst. Was ist passiert?
It's interesting you should say that, because …	Interessant, dass Sie das sagen, weil …
Talking about food, have you already tried the new Italian restaurant in the city centre?	Wo wir gerade über Essen sprechen: Haben Sie schon den neuen Italiener in der Innenstadt ausprobiert?
Changing the subject	**Das Thema wechseln**
I think it's best if we don't talk about politics.	Ich denke, es ist das Beste, wenn wir nicht über Politik sprechen.
If you don't mind, I'd rather not talk about that.	Wenn es Ihnen nichts ausmacht, würde ich lieber nicht darüber sprechen.
Yes … By the way, have you read …	Ja … Übrigens, haben Sie … gelesen?

Appendix | Phrases

Ending the conversation politely	Die Unterhaltung höflich beenden
Well, it's been good talking to you.	Nun, es war schön, mit Ihnen zu sprechen.
I suppose it's time to get back to work. See you around.	Ich denke, dass es Zeit ist, zur Arbeit zurückzukehren. Man sieht sich!
Excuse me, but I have just seen someone I need to speak to. It was nice talking to you.	Entschuldigen Sie, aber ich habe jemanden gesehen, mit dem ich sprechen muss. Es war nett, mit Ihnen zu reden.

Eating out	Essen gehen
Talking about preferences	**Über Vorlieben sprechen**
Do you eat meat / seafood / fish?	Essen Sie Fleisch / Meeresfrüchte / Fisch?
Do you like spicy food?	Mögen Sie scharfes Essen?
I'm a vegetarian / vegan.	Ich bin Vegetarier / Veganer.
I'm allergic to nuts.	Ich bin allergisch gegen Nüsse.
I'd prefer something light; I'm on a diet.	Ich würde etwas Leichtes bevorzugen – ich bin auf Diät.
I don't drink alcohol.	Ich trinke keinen Alkohol.
Talking about the menu	**Über die Speisekarte sprechen**
It's sweet / savoury / sour.	Es ist süß / herzhaft / sauer.
It's a starter / main dish / dessert.	Es ist ein(e) Vorspeise / Hauptgericht / Dessert.
What's in it?	Was ist da drin?
It's made of …	Es wird aus … gemacht.
It's boiled / fried / baked / roasted / filled with …	Es ist gekocht / gebraten / gebacken / geröstet / gefüllt mit …
Ordering	**Bestellen**
Are you ready to order?	Sind Sie bereit zum Bestellen?
As a starter, I'll take the … and then …	Als Vorspeise nehme ich …, und dann …
I'd like a side order of rice, please.	Ich hätte gerne (eine Portion) Reis als Beilage.
Shall we share a bottle of wine?	Sollen wir uns eine Flasche Wein teilen?
How do you like your steak? – Rare / medium / well-done, please.	Wie möchten Sie Ihr Steak? – Englisch / medium / durch, bitte.
What kind of wine / beer do you have?	Welche Weine / Biersorten haben Sie?
Talking about the food	**Über das Essen sprechen**
Enjoy your meal.	Guten Appetit!
How's your meal?	Wie ist Ihr Essen?
What's your … like?	Wie ist Ihr …?
The meat is very tender / a little tough.	Das Fleisch ist sehr zart / etwas zäh.
It's not as sweet as I expected.	Es ist nicht so süß, wie ich gedacht habe.
Excuse me, but my soup is cold.	Entschuldigen Sie, aber meine Suppe ist kalt.

Asking for the bill	Nach der Rechnung fragen
Excuse me, could we have the bill, please?	Entschuldigen Sie, könnten wir bitte die Rechnung haben?
Do you accept credit cards?	Akzeptieren Sie Kreditkarten?
This one's on me!	Das geht auf mich!
Shall we split the bill 50-50?	Sollen wir die Rechnung 50-50 teilen?

7 | Presentations

Beginning the presentation	Die Präsentation beginnen
I should like to start by telling you about my company.	Zunächst möchte ich Ihnen etwas über meine Firma sagen.
My presentation will deal with …	Meine Präsentation behandelt …
I intend to keep my presentation as brief as possible.	Ich möchte meine Präsentation so kurz wie möglich halten.
I would welcome any questions at the end of my presentation.	Ich wäre gern bereit, etwaige Fragen am Ende meiner Präsentation zu beantworten.
The handout summarises the main points and gives an overview of the relevant figures and statistics.	Das Handout enthält die Hauptpunkte und gibt einen Überblick über die entsprechenden Zahlen und Statistiken.
Structuring the main part of your presentation	**Den Hauptteil der Präsentation strukturieren**
Now my second point is …	Ich komme nun zu Punkt 2 …
Thirdly, let me give you some basic statistics.	Drittens darf ich Ihnen ein paar grundlegende Statistiken zeigen.
I should now like to move on to the next topic.	Ich möchte nun gern zum nächsten Thema übergehen.
An excellent example of this is …	Ein hervorragendes Beispiel dafür ist …
I should like to give you an example to illustrate this point.	Ich möchte diesen Punkt mit einem Beispiel erläutern.
Concluding your presentation	**Die Präsentation beenden**
To sum up we can say that …	Zusammenfassend kann man sagen, dass …
I should like to finish by saying / thanking the organisers / pointing out …	Ich möchte schließen mit der Bemerkung / dem Dank an die Organisatoren / dem Hinweis …
Are there any questions?	Gibt es Fragen?
Thank you for your attention.	Vielen Dank für Ihre Aufmerksamkeit.

Appendix | Phrases

8 | Dealing with customers

Making a complaint	Eine Beschwerde / Reklamation vorbringen
We are writing with reference to our order no. …	Wir nehmen Bezug auf unseren Auftrag Nr. …
On unpacking the cases our Incoming Goods Control discovered that 15 items are missing.	Beim Auspacken der Kisten stellte unsere Warenannahme fest, dass 15 Positionen fehlen.
We are afraid that several units are – seriously damaged / defective. – broken / badly scratched / stained.	Leider sind mehrere Teile – schwer beschädigt / schadhaft. – zerbrochen / stark zerkratzt / verschmutzt.
We are sorry to point out that the repair work has been poorly executed.	Wir müssen leider darauf hinweisen, dass die Reparatur schlecht ausgeführt wurde.
We believe the damage may be due to rough handling in transit.	Wir glauben, dass der Schaden auf unsachgemäße Behandlung beim Transport zurückzuführen ist.
This is very inconvenient for us because …	Dies kommt uns sehr ungelegen, da …
We would ask you to – replace the faulty goods at your expense. – grant us a price reduction of 10 %. – cut the price to € 550.	Wir möchten Sie bitten, – die mangelhafte Ware auf Ihre Kosten zu ersetzen. – uns einen Preisnachlass von 10 % zu gewähren. – den Preis auf € 550 zu senken.
We will keep the damaged goods until we hear from you.	Wir werden die beschädigten Waren behalten, bis wir von Ihnen hören.
Responding to a complaint	**Auf eine Beschwerde / Reklamation antworten**
Thank you for your email drawing a serious problem to our attention.	Danke für Ihre E-Mail, mit der Sie uns auf ein ernstes Problem aufmerksam gemacht haben.
We wish to apologise for this mistake.	Wir bitten für diesen Fehler um Entschuldigung.
We are extremely sorry for the poor service you have received.	Es tut uns außerordentlich leid, dass Sie einen unzureichenden Service erhalten haben.
We will investigate the matter thoroughly and inform you of the steps taken.	Wir werden die Angelegenheit gründlich untersuchen und Sie über die Schritte informieren, die wir unternommen haben.
Please return the faulty items at our expense.	Bitte senden Sie die mangelhaften Artikel auf unsere Kosten zurück.
We are prepared to reduce the price by 10 % if you decide to keep the goods.	Wir sind bereit, den Preis um 10 % zu senken, wenn Sie sich entschließen, die Ware zu behalten.
We hope that this proposal will find your approval.	Wir hoffen, dieser Vorschlag findet Ihre Zustimmung.

Audioscripts

A 1.1 Module 1 Meeting people, A 1, 2

Dialogue 1

Mr Neureuther: Neureuther, good morning.
Ms Hornbach: Good morning, Mr Neureuther.
Mr Neureuther: Good morning, Ms Hornbach.
Ms Hornbach: Mr Neureuther, the young man you were expecting from Denmark is here.
Mr Neureuther: Ah yes, please send him in. And Ms Hornbach, give Mr Dachs a call, will you please?
Ms Hornbach: I've already called him.
Christian: Hello, my name is Christian Eriksen. I come from Fanö in Denmark, and, uh, I'd like to work here as an intern for the next three months.
Mr Neureuther: Felix Neureuther. I'm the manager of the company.
Christian: Nice to meet you, Mr Neureuther.
Mr Neureuther: Nice to meet you too, Christian. I hope you had a pleasant trip.
Christian: Yes, it was fine, thank you. It's not far from Fanö to Kiel.
Mr Neureuther: Fine. Now, let me see, I guess you've handed all the necessary papers over to my secretary, Ms Hornbach?
Christian: Yes, I have.
Mr Neureuther: Oh good, Mr Dachs. I don't believe you've met Christian Eriksen. He'll be our new intern for the next three months. Christian, this is Mr Dachs, our personnel manager.
Mr Dachs: Nice to meet you Christian.
Christian: Nice to meet you too, Mr Dachs.
Mr Neureuther: Christian, Mr Dachs will take you to your team, so you can get to know them all. See you later, Christian.
Christian: See you later, Mr Neureuther.

Dialogue 2

Mr Dachs: Morning, everybody.
All of them: Good morning, Mr Dachs.
Mr Dachs: I'd like you to meet our new colleague. He'll be working with us for the next three months. He's in his second year of training. Christian, would you like to introduce yourself?
Christian: Hello, my name is Christian Eriksen. I come from Fanö, that's an island off the coast of Denmark. The company I work for is a bit smaller than yours; there's just the boss, a skilled worker and two trainees.
Silke: Hi Christian, nice to meet you. My name is Silke, and I'm also in my second year of training.
Christian: Nice to meet you too, Silke. I'm glad you speak English, because my German is not so fluent. But I'm doing my best to improve.
Silke: No problem, we'll manage.
Josef: Hello Christian, I'm Josef, but everybody calls me Joe. I'm your foreman. My English is not perfect, but Silke can always help. I've been here for quite a long time. Isn't that right, Mr Dachs?
Mr Dachs: Yes, Joe has been with us for over 20 years now. I think for the first few weeks you'll work with him. Well, let's get back to work now. If you have any questions, you can ask Joe, but you can always come to my office, too.
Christian: Thank you, Mr Dachs.

A 1.2 Module 2 Your company, A 4

Herr Kirchner: OK, so we've covered human resources, accounting, sales and marketing, and purchasing. Now we come to the more technical side of the company, and – of course – the area where you will be spending your time. OK, do you have any questions before we continue?
Sean: Yes, just a general question really. How old is the company?
Herr Kirchner: Older than you, Sean, that's for sure! Krone Elektronik was founded by Dr Florian Krone in 1954, and is still a family-owned company to this day.
Sean: And is this the headquarters here in Bochum?
Herr Kirchner: Yes, it is. Krone has nine manufacturing plants and sales offices across Europe, but this is the largest. In fact, we also have two in the USA – in Chicago and Baltimore.
Sean; Are there any plants in Great Britain?
Herr Kirchner: No, there's not. But we are opening a new factory in South Korea next year.
Sean: And how many people work for Krone Elektronik?

Herr Kirchner: That's a good question, Sean. I don't know the exact number, but it is at least 10,000, if you include the USA. OK, let's go on with the tour, shall we? The building to your right is our research and development department. They are currently working on a new braking system for a major German car company.

Sean: And what goes on in the large building next to it?

Herr Kirchner: This is our main building, which has three functions. Firstly, it is where production planners work – and this is where you will spend most of your time. Their job is to optimize the manufacturing process by keeping production times and costs down. Secondly, as you can see, here are also the production halls, where you will start your internship.

Sean: You mentioned three functions. So what else happens over there? It's a really big place.

Herr Kirchner: Yes, it's over 6,000 square metres. Those people you can see over there are responsible for quality control. They test all of the components and devices before they go to the customer.

Sean: How many components are made here in Bochum?

Herr Kirchner: Well, one of the main components we produce here are the cylinder heads, and we make thousands of them every year. And each and every one of them must be inspected by the guys in quality control.

Sean: I guess that's an important job. I'm really looking forward to getting to work.

Herr Kirchner: That's great. I will introduce you to the foreman this afternoon. OK, finally, behind this building we have the IT department. At the moment, they are very busy dealing with the problems caused by our new operating system.

Sean: Oh, that doesn't sound too good. What exactly is the problem?

Herr Kirchner: I'm not sure exactly, some kind of interface difficulties, I think. OK, let's go into the canteen and have some lunch, shall we? Then I can answer some more of your questions.

⊙ A 1.3 Module 3 Telephoning, B 5

Alex: Fertighaus Henke, Alex Bauder.
Caller: Yes, hello. Do you speak English?
Alex: Er, yes, a little. How can I help you?
Caller: Well, my name is Matthew Reid and your company is currently building my house. I'm a little confused. I thought this was Mr Deschler's telephone number. He is the construction manager, isn't he?
Alex: Yes, he is, but unfortunately he is off sick today, so all of his calls are being diverted to me. Can I help you with something?
Caller: Well, I was calling to give Mr Deschler some changes to our house.
Alex: OK, and what was your name again, please?
Caller: Reid, Matthew Reid.
Alex: Could you possibly spell that please?
Caller: Certainly. It's R-E-I-D.
Alex: R-I-E-D.
Caller: No, R-E for England, I for India, D.
Alex: Sorry, R-E-I-D. OK, Mr Reid, and what is the address of the house?
Caller: Well, so far it is only a foundation pit, but it is Ringstrasse 26 in Lernsdorf.
Alex: Ringstrasse 26, Lernsdorf. Ah, yes, I know the site. We are scheduled to begin on your cellar next week, I think. OK, if you give me the information, I will pass it on to Mr Deschler. Let me just find a piece of paper ... OK, I'm ready.
Caller: First of all, in the kitchen we need to move the extractor fan twenty centimetres to the left, so that it is directly over the hob. And the hole needs to have a diameter of one hundred and eighty-four millimetres, and we also need ...
Alex: Sorry Mr Reid, but I am afraid any changes to your kitchen need to be discussed with the kitchen fitters. Are there any changes to the plans for any other part of the house?
Caller: Er, just a moment. Let me look at my list. OK, we need to change the height of the toilets in the bathroom. At the moment they are planned to be forty-five centimetres and we would like them to be fifty. Plus, we need to add another two hundred and twenty volt socket to the right of the bathroom mirror for my electric razor.
Alex: OK, anything else?
Caller: Yes, my wife and I have decided that we will need a larger carport. I have spoken to a friend and he says we should make it eight metres by six metres by three metres. Can you find out how much extra this would cost, please?
Alex: Of course. Let me just confirm, eight metres long by six metres wide. And how high should it be?

Caller: Three metres high. Of course, this means that we will have a smaller garden, but I think a carport is very useful. You can also ask Mr Deschler how big our garden will be with the new carport. It is currently one hundred and thirty-five square metres.
Alex: OK, I will ask him to adjust the plan and get in touch with you as soon as he is back in the office.
Caller: That's great. Oh, just one more thing. My wife wants to put larger windows in the living room. At the moment, they are one hundred and forty-eight centimetres by one hundred and eleven in the plan. She would like them to be one hundred and eighty-six by two hundred and twenty-two.
Alex: One eight six by two two two. OK Mr Reid, I will pass this information on to Mr Deschler and ask him to give you a call. Does he have your telephone number?
Caller: Yes, I think so, but let me give you my work number, too. It is 0391 587660… Thank you for your help Mr Bauder. Goodbye.
Alex: You're welcome Mr Reid. Goodbye.

⊙ A 1.4 Module 5 Applications, C 1

Andrea: Hi David, how are you doing?
David: Hi Andrea. I'm fine thanks. How are you?
Andrea: Yeah, I'm OK. Busy, but fine.
David: I heard that you were thinking about applying for a three-month internship in the Northampton branch. Is that true?
Andrea: Yes, that's right. I really want to spend some time in England. I guess it was the same with you and coming to Germany.
David: Exactly. I wanted to see how things worked over here. So, you want to spend some time with my old colleagues, eh? That's great.
Andrea: Well actually, I wanted to ask you for a bit of advice if that's OK with you?
David: Sure, what can I help you with?
Andrea: Well, I have to officially apply for the internship, which means a letter and a CV.
David: OK, would you like me to read your letter?
Andrea: Yes, that would be great. I am going to finish it this weekend, and then I will bring it to work on Monday. Thanks. But where I really need your advice is with the CV. I was wondering if you had any tips for me. I know there are some differences between German and English CVs.
David: Yes, there are, you're right. Hmm … tips … let me see. OK, the first thing to remember is that your CV should be no longer than two pages.
Andrea: Two pages, OK.
David: Also, make sure you use good-quality paper and never send your CV without a covering letter.
Andrea: OK …
David: And don't forget to highlight your strengths and achievements. And when you talk about your work experience, start with your most recent job.
Andrea: Do I need to include a picture?
David: In England, a CV does not have a picture, but you can have one if you like. What is important is that you include the name and contact details of two references. These could be a supervisor, or maybe a teacher.
Andrea: OK, great. Anything else?
David: Yeah, make sure that everything you write in your CV is the truth. If you are asked to explain something during the interview and you can't, then it will be pretty embarrassing. Be confident and sell yourself, but don't lie. Er … once you have finished the CV, read through it and check the spelling and the grammar. The best thing to do is to give it to a friend. And, when you send it, keep a copy for yourself to read before the interview.
Andrea: Thanks a lot for the advice, David. Thanks a lot, I'm really grateful.
David: Don't mention it, Andrea. Let me know if there is anything else I can do.
Andrea: Well … you did say somebody should read over it and check everything – and who'd be better than a native speaker …?

⊙ A 1.5 Module 6 Socialising, A 1

Fabian: Hi, I'm Fabian.
Jan: Hello Fabian, my name's Jan. I'm with the group from Warsaw, Poland.
Fabian: Welcome to our company. Is this your first visit to Germany?
Jan: Actually, I've been here before. But my German isn't very good.
Fabian: Don't worry, we can talk in English. I should really practice more anyway. How was your trip? Was it a long journey?
Jan: No, not really. We took the plane from Warsaw to Stuttgart. Then someone from your company met us at the airport.

Fabian: Jan, would you like something to drink: coffee, juice, lemonade?

Jan: Sure, a lemonade would be good.

Fabian: OK, let's go to our canteen and sit down for a while.

Fabian: Here we go; I hope it's cold enough.

Jan: Thanks. So, I guess that you are also a trainee. What year are you in?

Fabian: I'm in my third year. What about you?

Jan: I've just started. How many trainees are there in your company?

Fabian: Er … about ten, I think.

Jan: That's quite a lot. There are only three trainees in our company, all in metal engineering. I think your company is much bigger than ours.

Fabian: Yeah, we even have our own football team. We don't play in a league; it's just for fun.

Jan: That sounds great! You should visit us in Poland one day. Maybe we could arrange a match.

Fabian: That's a good idea. Are you a football fan?

Jan: Yeah. I don't play myself, but I like to watch.

Fabian: Which team do you like?

Jan: Manchester United.

Fabian: Really? They're my favourite team, too! Well, apart from VFB Stuttgart, of course.

Jan: Do you live in Stuttgart?

Fabian: No, I live in a small town nearby. I have to take the bus every morning. But when the weather's good, I can take my motorbike.

Jan: Cool! Unfortunately I don't have a motorbike. I get a lift from a colleague who works in the same department as me.

Fabian: What do you do in your free time?

Jan: I like going to clubs, and sometimes I go fishing with my friends. What about you? Playing football, I suppose.

Fabian: Yeah, football and riding my motorbike.

⊙ A 1.6 Module 7 Presentations, C 1

Good morning ladies and gentlemen. Today I would like to present our new range of wooden furniture, *Simply Wood*. The range, which is shown here on the first slide, includes chairs, a large table, a lounger, and benches. I would like to start by talking about the materials used in the furniture. All of the *Simply Wood* range is made from single softwood timber and has been hand-crafted by our highly-skilled carpenters and joiners. If you look at this picture, you can see that the benches and the seats are designed with a low back, deep seats and long arms to offer a great deal of comfort and convenience. Thanks to a special varnish, the furniture is 100 % weatherproof and will not suffer from discolouring. As you can see from this final slide, the furniture is also available in white, to give it a classic, timeless look. And do not worry, we have used a durable, white polyurethane coating that is suitable for every environment. On your handout you will see more details about each piece, including measurements. Thank you for your attention this morning.
Are there any questions? Yes …

⊙ A 1.7 Module 8 Dealing with customers, A 4

Answering machine: Guten Tag. Sie sind mit Stefan Bauder verbunden. Leider bin ich im Moment nicht erreichbar. Bitte hinterlassen Sie eine Nachricht nach dem Ton. Danke!

Brian: Hello Mr Bauder, this is Brian Jenkins calling from New Wave Marketing in Hamburg. I am calling about the new IT network that your technicians set up last week. Unfortunately, we have been experiencing some problems. Since your technicians were here, some employees have had difficulty connecting to the Internet, and others have no access to our network at all and cannot even log on to their computers! However, the worst thing is that some important files and documents seem to have been lost as a result of the migration to the new software. One of these files was a presentation for a very important client. This is a particular problem for us because we have a meeting with this client on Monday, and we need the presentation and do not have enough time to redo it. Could you please look into this problem for us urgently as time is running out? If we do not hear from you by the end of today, we will have to look elsewhere. I will be in meetings this afternoon, but you can contact me per e-mail under B dot Jenkins at NWM…de. Thank you.

Video scripts

🎧 V 1 Company Tour

Markus Smith: This is the accounting department… and this is where customer service is.

Ralf Kramer: Do most of the calls come from the local area?

MS: Actually no, far from it. Because we deliver to more than thirty-five countries, our staff speaks a wide variety of languages. So SAND Machinery's customer service is able to respond 24 hours a day, 7 days a week to our clients' needs – around the globe and around the clock.

RK: Impressive.

MS: Well, Mr Kramer, that's an overview of our main building. We've been through the purchasing department, human resources, accounting department and customer service.
Do you have any questions so far?

RK: Well, it's been interesting to see how things are structured here. Thanks again for taking me around and explaining everything. Actually, I do have one question: Which building is my internship in?

MS: Ha. That's on the next tour. We'll go through the production planning department, our production facilities, as well as quality control. That's all in the next building. There you'll see where the finished products are inspected and also meet the head of your department.
This is our cafeteria. May I offer you a coffee?

RK: Yes, please.

MS: Right this way.

RK: Thank you.

MS: Here you are.

RK: Thank you.

MS: You're welcome.

RK: Could you give me a brief overview of my tasks during the internship?

MS: Of course. You'll be supporting staff as well as generally helping to prepare for the IT update. We plan on installing software on our machines next month.

RK: Good. I'm eager to get in and get my feet wet.

MS: I see.

RK: Do you mind if I ask a few more questions?

MS: Of course not. That's why I'm here.

RK: What's the total size of SAND Machinery's workforce?

MS: Our permanent full-time staff numbers three hundred and fifteen employees.
Also we have an additional fifty employees who work part-time.

RK: Does the company have other sites as well?

MS: Yes, we have a larger production site on the outskirts of town with many industrial technicians who ensure that the production process runs smoothly. They produce wiring, conduits, circuit boards and alternators.

RK: That sounds interesting.

MS: If you're finished, I'd like to show you where you'll be working.

RK: Certainly.

MS: Unless you have any more questions.

RK: No, not at the moment. But I'm sure I'll have plenty as we go…

MS: Ok.

🎧 V 2 Telephoning

Ralf Kramer: Hello. This is Ralf Kramer at J.Z. Sports. How may I help you?

Bob Squire: Hi. Bob Squire from E-Mobility Xperteez here. I'm returning a call from Mr. Deeds. Can I please speak to him?

RK: Um… Excuse me, could you please repeat that? The connection is very bad.

BS: Ah, right… All right… Sorry… My name is Bob Squire from E-Mobility Xperteez. I spoke with Mr. Deeds from your office about an hour ago. He rang me up regarding our new E-mobility vehicles. I couldn't answer everything then, but now I have all the details he asked for.

RK: Ah, yes, my boss… He's in a meeting at the moment. Could he call you back?

BS: Unfortunately I'm leaving the office very soon. I'll be out of the office for a week.

RK: Oh… Maybe you could set up an appointment for when you return.

BS: Actually, I'd rather leave a message for Mr. Deeds, if that's possible? He needs the technical information about our E-Mobility vehicles as soon as possible.

RK: Yes, but if you could send him an email, he might get the information faster. He always has access to his emails.

BS: Our mail server is having problems today. It keeps crashing. I would prefer to give you the information now over the phone. Could you please write it down and pass it on to him?

RK: Could you speak up, please? I can hardly hear you. There's so much background noise.

BS: I'm sorry… I'm sorry. My mobile is having signal problems. I said I have to give you the information now.

RK: Okay, no problem. Could you please repeat your name for me?

BS: That's Bob Squire.

RK: How do you spell your name?

BS: S-Q-U-I-R-E. Now Mr. Deeds wants the figures for our model with the 54 kw engine. He already knows the height, length and weight.

RK: Yes, that's right.

BS: He wanted to know if the vehicle could reach 155 km per hour and was suitable for long journeys. The answer to both questions is yes.

RK: Ah, good.

BS: You can travel a distance of 200 km or more on a single charge.

RK: Could you repeat that number for me again?

BS: 200 km. Make sure to specify that's in kilometres and not miles, so there is no misunderstanding. And also make a note that the capacity of the battery is greater than those available one year ago, and the new model can go almost twice as fast.

RK: I'll let him know, thank you. Is there anything else?

BS: No, that's it for now. If Mr. Deeds has any further questions he can call me. I'll be back in the office on the 15th.

RK: Okay, I'll let him know. So thank you for your call and all the information.

BS: You're welcome. Goodbye.

RK: Bye, bye.

V 3 Job interview

Glen Smith: Hello Mr. Smithers.
Paul Smithers: Hello.
GS: Welcome to Ostico.
PS: Thank you.
GS: It's nice to meet you.
PS: Nice to meet you, too.
GS: Please come in. Please have a seat. May I offer you some coffee or water?
PS: No, thank you.
GS: I hope your journey from Germany was a pleasant one.
PS: Yes. The flight was fine, thank you.
GS: Good. Now, Mr. Smithers, you are applying for the team leader position currently available in our IT department. As I said in my email, your CV stands out from the other applicants. Perhaps you could tell me a little more about yourself and your qualifications for the position?
PS: Well, I was born in Cologne. I studied informatics in Aachen. For two years I worked in Boston as a technical project manager for a large software company. I was a specialist for mobile solutions and during my time there I acquired strong programming skills and a solid knowledge of project management.
GS: That's wonderful. Could you tell me a little about the job before that?
PS: Yes, I worked for a large telecommunications company in Bonn. I held that job for three years before I got the offer from the US.
GS: Your reference from the departmental head Mr Geiger says that you were an outstanding worker.
PS: Yes, they were very satisfied with my work.
GS: Can you tell me what your greatest strength is?
PS: I would say that I'm a good team player and that I'm good at making decisions.
GS: That's fine. Could you please share with me what you already know about Ostico?
PS: Well, your company specializes in innovative mobile solutions for all devices. Ostico establishes the highest levels of functionality among existing style and coding standards. The company was founded seven years ago. Today over 350 people work for Ostico and you have customers in Europe, Asia and the US.
GS: Oh, you are well informed. What would make you a good candidate for our team?
PS: I have the ability to motivate others and also a strong desire to find creative solutions for clients' needs.
GS: And what is your greatest weakness?

PS: I am a perfectionist and always think there is a better way of doing things. I'm not afraid to try out new ideas and concepts.

GS: I see. Well, I think in this environment that kind of weakness could be an advantage. After all, we want to develop the perfect mobile solutions for our clients.

PS: Well, you can be assured that I'll do my best!

GS: That sounds good. I think you've answered all my questions. Do you have any of your own?

PS: Yes, when do you think you will make your decision?

GS: We'll call within a week. Is there anything else?

PS: Yes, how many people would I be responsible for?

GS: There are six people on the team. If you like, I can take you over and introduce you to them now.

PS: Yes, that would be great.

GS: Ok, great. Please follow me. The IT department is this way.

V 4 Technical support

Jane Butterworth: IT department. Jane Butterworth speaking. How can I help you?

Paul Smithers: Hello, my name is Paul Smithers. I am having some trouble with my PC. I'm unable to get online and my scanner doesn't work. I hope you can help me out.

JB: I'd be happy to, Mr. Smithers. Can you tell me a little bit more about your problem? Let's start with the online connection. What happens when you try to go online?

PS: Well, nothing happens. Last night before I went home it was fine, but now when I try to open the browser … well … nothing happens.

JB: Have you tried rebooting the system?

PS: How do I do that? It sounds like you want me to kick the machine. Believe me, I'd love to but…

JB: No, no, Mr. Smithers, I can appreciate that feeling, but that's not what I mean by rebooting. When you reboot the system, you turn off the computer completely, you disconnect all external devices and hard drives. Then, you wait a minute before turning the computer back on again.

PS: Oh, okay… I have already rebooted it three times and it hasn't helped.

JB: What about the modem? Have you done the same with the modem?

PS: Which modem?

JB: It's the small box that should be connected to your PC by a small cable or by a wireless link within your computer.

PS: Oh, you mean that little white box with the green light in the hallway by the printer everybody in the office shares? That box?

JB: Sure. That sounds right. Try turning it off. Then wait a minute before turning it on again.

PS: Okay. Can you hold the line?

JB: Sure.

PS: Ms. Butterworth?

JB: Yes. How did that work out?

PS: Great! I'm back online. That was it.

JB: Good. Now, when you try to use the scanner, do you get an error message saying that there is something wrong with the scanner's software? Or is it a hardware issue?

PS: I didn't get any message. I tried to scan a blueprint but it didn't work. Normally it arrives as a pdf file in the scandocs folder on my PC.

JB: Have you checked to see that the device is properly connected?

PS: Um, no. … Not yet. … Oh, yes! Now the scanner is back and responding.

JB: Excellent. Is there anything else I can help you with?

PS: No, everything's fixed now. Thank you very much.

JB: I'm glad, I could help. Feel free to call me any time.

PS: Thank you very much again.

JB: You're welcome.

PS: Goodbye.

JB: Bye, bye.

V 5 Waste – The future's most valuable resource

Voiceover: The waste produced by our consumer society is collected, separated, recycled or disposed of. In Germany, this amounts to several 100 million tons of rubbish a year. The question used to be how to best dispose of waste. These days, however, the resources it holds are becoming ever more valuable. Businesses around the globe are competing for something many people regard as worthless. These days, rubbish is a billion-euro industry.

Klaus Wiemer: There's an ongoing battle for rubbish. Many people see it as modern urban warfare.

Voiceover: Today businesses are protecting their rubbish by any means possible. Despite extensive security measures, more than 20 tons of copper were stolen right here this year. The reason: the copper supply is limited but can be recycled indefinitely without detriment to its quality. It's one of the raw materials that emerging nations like China and India are eager to get their hands on. They're prepared to pay a high price tag for our rubbish.

Klaus Wiemer: The global struggle for raw materials has greatly surpassed what it was in the past. This is because it is much less expensive than it once was to ship one ton of a given raw material to China. The distance the product has to travel is no longer a prime consideration. The price structure and demand for raw materials are.

Voiceover: Does that mean rubbish will one day be among our most important resources for producing energy? One ton of residual waste can produce the same amount of heat as 200 litres of oil, making it highly desirable. In the last three decades, energy consumption has increased by around 66 percent, and natural raw materials are getting scarcer all the time.

Daniel Goldmann: It's entirely conceivable that people will pay money to acquire specific types of rubbish. We no longer live in an age where waste is in great surplus and disposal is our only concern; those days are long gone. Once rubbish is viewed as a raw material, the question is: How do I get my hands on it? If this were the case, people would have to compete for various sorts of rubbish.

Voiceover: Our waste is getting a second lease on life. Around the world, scientists are investigating means of resource recovery. Recycling is more than just environmental protection. The global economy's demand for waste is sky-high.

V 6 Pipe inspection

Voiceover: Pipelines allow us to transport oil and natural gas over long distances. Regular inspections are performed to ensure the pipes don't leak. It's these two men's job to watch the tube every day. They investigate the interior of gas and oil lines with what are called pipeline pigs. Unlike the name might suggest, these high-tech machines move through liquid substances, and there are different types. Some creep along using brushes and are simply mounted on an engine device that power[s] them through the pipes as they clean them. Others are brimming with analytical technology.

This pig is being prepared to make an inspection trip. The over 2-metre-long vehicle travels through the pipes at up to 10 metres a second. Along the way, it's got to inspect more than a hundred metres of pipe, looking for weak spots, often only a few millimetres in size. The pig is sent into the pipeline on special guides.

The inspection device uses magnetic fields to identify vulnerable points. In theory, the pipe is of the same thickness at every point. The magnetic field changes where the pipe is thinner. The pig manages 300 km in just under 2 days. Over this time it's powered by high-performance batteries. The data [sic] is read immediately using a standard firewire cable.

Pigs are deployed all over the world, so they have to be able to withstand the minus 40 degrees centigrade of Alaska just as well as they do the plus 60 degrees of Mexico.

The readings from pipeline inspections in Europe, South America and Africa are analyzed in Oldenzaal, Holland.

Holger Hennerkes: If we look at a length of approximately a hundred metres – it's the normal length of the inspection of such a pipeline – this creates about 100 gigabytes of data. These data are stored on flash memory devices, as we all are accustomed to from an everyday digital camera. From there they are transferred to a special program. Our data evaluation experts then depict these data, using special colour-coded diagrams and line diagrams, and then you can identify the sections where metal has probably grown thinner.

The pig has stored the data using a grid that's accurate to within 2.5–6 millimetres. The blue bands are welding seams or junctions. They help the experts to orientate themselves. In this case, the evaluation shows that the pipe has become thinner.

Holger Hennerkes: You might, for example, think that corrosion has ensued and caused this thinning of the metal, i.e. that corrosion or rust has taken place on the interior or the exterior of the pipeline. And in these areas, the strength of the outer wall has been compromised. But it's also possible that exterior influences – it could have been excavator tools during construction work, or something similar – have caused the damage, and that this has left scratches that lead to these problem areas. Our specialists are able to determine the exact length and width of these defects, and to inform our customers of them.

Voiceover: The number of surface defects varies greatly. There can be over a thousand defects on a 100-km stretch of piping. The machine provides the data, but having to make the decision about whether to investigate a spot more closely or not is down to people.

V 7 High voltage work

Voiceover: Calm and sunny – perfect conditions for these linesmen. Only with optimal weather conditions will the helicopters ferry these men to their workplace in the sky. Their job is to repair the damaged overhead power lines of Europe's electrical grid. These high-voltage lines carry 380,000 volts of electricity. When the helicopter teams fly to repair a line, only the neighbouring cables are switched off; the rest remain at full voltage. To make the job a little safer, the cables that have been switched off are also earthed. Despite such precautions, concentration is the name of the game.

Gunther Blasack: This sort of mission is never routine. Every flight's completely different; no two jobs are ever the same. Things change from one place to the next, and you've got to decide how to fly your mission accordingly.

Voiceover: The helicopter's undergoing final preparations. As it's being refuelled, the men run through their strategy once more; any mistakes here could be deadly.

The linesmen are transported to the faulty line in a steel basket affixed to the helicopter. They won't set foot on the ground till their mission is complete. The team is in constant contact with the central control room, where the affected power lines are turned on and off. Only once they've been disabled, can the team start work. This kind of mission places great demands upon the pilot. Gunter Blasack used to fly rescue missions and is well aware of the dangers this kind of job poses. He's run through the emergency situations thousands of times in his head.

Gunther Blasack: In extreme situations – say, the basket got caught up in the overhead lines – I can't just parachute out and save my own skin. The people down there depend upon me bringing them home safely.

Voiceover: A regular patrol team only recently discovered the damaged overhead line. The damage probably occurred during a thunderstorm. Meanwhile, the police have blocked the road to prevent any accidents. The team can finally get to work. The linesmen have to work quickly: Shutting down overhead power lines costs millions.

The men attach a coil of aluminium wire to repair the line. After 15 minutes the job is complete, and it's time for the team to fly back to base, refuel, and start all over again. They have five more cables to repair today. The fixed line is switched back on and electricity flows through it once more. The quicker the lines are repaired, the better; a drop in supply can have serious consequences. If there's no back-up grid, a power cut can quickly bring an entire city to its knees.

V 8 Ras Laffan

Voiceover: Until the early 1990s, Ras Laffan was little more than an idyllic stretch of beach some 80 km from the Qatari capital, Doha. Today, it's home to an enormous industrial complex processing the nation's natural gas. It's hard to believe, but typical of Qatar's rapid economic development in recent years.

Each year, millions of tons of natural gas are processed at the port of Ras Laffan, and there are plans to more than double the size of the complex over the coming years. This means that not only is Ras Laffan a massive industrial plant, but it's also one of the largest construction sites in the world. Thousands of construction workers from more than 40 countries are busy welding together enormous steel pipes, building gigantic gas storage tanks in the sand, and assembling huge steel structures. The wind, and above all the high temperatures, push the workers to their limits. Concrete, for example, has to be cooled using ice-cold water; otherwise it would never set in the 50 °C heat.

Ras Laffan is one of the fastest growing industrial regions in the world. Among the cranes, enormous installations process the country's most precious commodity. From here ships will transport Qatar's natural gas all over the world.

To allow the gas to be transported more easily and efficiently, it's cooled to minus 162 °C. At this temperature, the gas becomes a liquid. As a result, its volume is decreased by a factor of 600. Without this procedure the transport costs would be immense. The cooling process is achieved in a number of stages involving massive cooling plants. The amount of energy needed to cool the gas is enormous. The equivalent of 15 % of the gas's energy is used up by cooling and transportation alone.

The industrial region Ras Laffan covers an area of 106 square kilometres, and as demand for Qatar's liquid gold grows, so too is the likelihood that the Ras Laffan industrial complex will do the same.

V 9 Pipelines

Voiceover: Pipelines are put under tremendous strain. They need to have a long life span and should require as little maintenance as possible. That's why they're subjected to the most stringent quality-control checks from day one. The pipes, which will carry oil and gas over hundreds of kilometres, are made from a special alloy: Steel mixed with niobium and titanium is a popular choice.

The machines, which have to shape steel plates up to 4 cm thick, need tremendous power. When subjected to 60,000 tons, the steel bends like a blade of grass.

Forming a round pipe from flat steel sheets requires a number of processes. At the same time, the pipes can only differ by a few tenths of a millimetre.

Here the pipes are being pre-welded and fused together. The submerged arc-welding technique employed in this factory ensures that the steel plates are firmly bound together. The mechanized expander gives the pipes their final shape. The expander exerts a mind-boggling 1500 tons of force. Electronic eyes then check every joint and weld using ultrasound and radiography.

But even now, the pipe still isn't complete. The inner walls of gas pipes are given a special coating, allowing the gas to travel through the pipeline as smoothly as possible.

Pipes destined for use in offshore pipelines are given an additional outer casing of concrete. And this serves two functions: First, it gives the pipe extra weight so that it sinks to the sea bed when being laid. Second, it offers an extra level of protection against the elements. These pipelines are subjected to extreme conditions. The pressure in gas pipelines, for example, can reach 200 bar or more. In the case of offshore pipelines, the entire pipeline is ravaged by waves and strong currents.

Approximately 3 million kilometres worth of oil and gas pipelines currently crisscross the globe, but that's just the beginning; 25,000 kilometres of new pipes are being laid each year.

V 10 Robots in the hospital

Voiceover: Robotic couriers: Every modern hospital has silent helpers such as these. They make sure things behind the scenes run smoothly. At the Jena University Hospital in Germany, 24 of these robotic couriers whiz through the hospital. They travel via their own lift-and-tunnel system. This allows them to run errands while going unnoticed by patients and visitors.

A central computer determines the path each courier travels. It communicates with the individual vehicles via infrared data transmitters, passing on individual delivery orders. Each transport vehicle has the entire routing system programmed into its computer memory. The battery-powered couriers use magnets that are detected by sensors to navigate. They assist in righting the vehicles' paths should they lose their way.

The main task they perform is transporting wheeled containers. Four hundred containers are being transported throughout the hospital at any given time. Half of them are used solely to carry food. In the meantime, these inconspicuous silver carriages have become high-tech kitchen assistants. Every day, two and a half thousand lunches are prepared here. So they don't have to keep the meals warm for hours on end, the kitchen staff cooks them the day before and lets them cool. Special plates, with a layer containing silver, allow them to heat them up easily and serve them fresh and hot to patients when mealtime comes around. The bottoms of the plates are heated up by the tray holders which are equipped with inductor coils. They produce alternating magnetic fields that heat up the coated dishes. The robot couriers transport the state-of-the-art containers to the wards; the hospital staff takes over from there. However, the robots can also perform food distribution and transport patients.

Prof. Klaus Höffken: I can't conceive of us doing that – that we would transport patients on carts, like they sometimes do in airports, where you have to search around, confused, until you find the right terminal. We won't do that in the hospital. Here, we have people in need. We have a social responsibility in our job, and that's that. This hospital transports around 700 patients a day, but here in Jena, that will continue to be done by people …

V 11 Portable power stations

Voiceover: Often there are times out in the open when you could do with a little bit of power, either for electric fencing or for, say, an alarm system on a remote barn. But it could be a long way to lay a cable, and if you're using batteries, well, you've got to take them all the way back again to get them recharged. So how about this? This is a portable, 12-volt power station. It uses both wind energy and solar power, so it's totally green. It's a British invention; it costs around about £400, and it produces enough electricity for 6 miles of cabling. And you could plug in a lamp or a mobile phone. And now the inventor's looking for a firm to produce the power station under licence.

V 12 Car speed control

Voiceover: We enjoy speed but speed is one of the most important factors in serious accidents. Speed kills. Over 3,500 people die in road accidents in the UK every year, and 320,000 are injured. Well over half of us exceed the speed limit, given the chance; the faster the driver goes, the greater the chance of losing control and the less time he has to react if anything does go wrong. Just a 5-mile-an-hour increase in the speed of traffic can lead to a 25% greater chance of injury accidents.

Work in progress at the Motor Industry Research Association (MIRA) could make speeding a thing of the past. Research funded by the British government could see speed-controlled cars on British roads within the decade. And this isn't just a warning to the driver, but an intelligent system that will ride along with the driver, making sure that the car obeys speed limits. The driver has no choice in the matter.

As this car approaches a local speed-limit sign, its on-board satellite positioning system makes sure that the car's engine and braking systems slow down, well before it reaches the speed-restriction sign.

Driver: The sensation is just like putting your foot to the floor, but there's no change, and you can't feel anything, no acceleration at all.

Voiceover: Millions of otherwise law-abiding citizens commit criminal acts every day by breaking the speed limit. Speed control is never popular with motorists or motor manufacturers, who rely heavily on the subliminal image of fast cars to sell new products. Speed cameras initially led to a dramatic reduction in speeding, but now most drivers only slow down briefly when they spot a camera. Electronic speed control could signal the end of getaway cars and joyriders, but eventually it would also do away with the loathed speed cameras and speeding prosecutions. The MIRA car speed-control technology works on the road, but the next step is to find out how drivers cope with the system, and whether it has any safety disadvantages. The University of Leeds has built a simulator and is testing driver behaviours, using a model of a real journey. Initial work on the simulator shows that it does reflect drivers' behaviour on the road. During the journey, the guinea-pig driver is faced with a number of driving situations. The researchers want to find out whether the control system changes the driver's behaviour. If the driver is frustrated by having this speed control, will his behaviour become more reckless in other manoeuvres?

Driver: This stretch of, um, road that we're driving now is – we actually use it for the validation experiment on the simulator. It's actually a stretch of – oops! bit too quick – a stretch of real road from the A614 in Humberside. Uh, we took the Ordnance Survey data for the road, modelled it [sic] up in the simulator, obviously went out to the real road to take pictures of the buildings so we could create the same images within the simulator, and then we could obviously use a like-for-like comparison. We had cameras set up on the real road looking at people's speed and lane position, and then obviously we could do the same in the simulator, and do a one-for-one comparison. This is quite an annoying part, it's going even slower; it's going about 40 miles per hour compared to the 60 miles per hour speed limit. And obviously the road markings don't allow me to pass. Now this goes on, this event, for 3 or 4 minutes; it's just to see when the person gets so sick of following this car that they actually will commit a violation to cross the double white line, which for me is now.

Voiceover: So far, the results on the simulator are encouraging. The speed-control system has few negative effects, far fewer than drivers themselves anticipated. But the larger question is: Will drivers accept it?

Speaker 1: Drivers like to speed. Um, they get a thrill out of speeding, they get to their destinations more quickly, and obviously, most of the time we're on the road we want to minimize the time that we're taking to get somewhere. Drivers don't like being forced to comply with the speed limit; they don't like whatever way you do it. They don't like traffic calming, they don't like speed cameras, and they don't like something that stops the car from being driven above the speed limit. They lose their freedom, if you like.

Speaker 2: That's not good, is it?! When a car travels so fast, you want to put your foot down and go! When you're in a rush, isn't it?!

Speaker 3: It's probably a more positive way of controlling speed than what we're currently – the method that we're currently using.

Voiceover: Government is trying to make speeding as socially unacceptable as drink-driving has become. Electronic speed control could become a life-saver.

Speaker 1: Our best estimate of the injury accident savings is that we would save 35% of injury accidents, and the same calculation indicates we'd save almost two thirds of fatal accidents across the country. That's a dramatic improvement.

Speaker 4: Anything for safety, carry on with me. Spend what they like, do what they like, as long as it's for safety.

Voiceover: Research indicates that it would save fuel, and dramatically reduce traffic congestion as well. The recommended plan is to phase in this speed-control system in the UK over the next two decades. It would be voluntary at first, but would later become mandatory in new cars.

Grammar overview

Present Tense (Gegenwart)

Bildung: Present Tense (simple)		
Merke: Bei der 3. Person Einzahl *(he / she / it)* wird ein *s* an die Endung des Verbs angehängt.	I **like** / you **like** / he (she / it) **likes** we **like** / you **like** / they **like**	computer games.

Verwendung: Present Tense (simple)	
- bei allgemein bekannten Tatsachen und Aussagen - bei regelmäßigen Handlungen: Schlüsselwörter: *usually, normally, always, never, sometimes, often…* - bei Gewohnheiten - bei Fahrplänen, Öffnungszeiten etc. für die Zukunft	- Most cars run on petrol. - I usually start work at 7 o'clock. - He doesn't smoke. - My train leaves at 10 o'clock tomorrow morning.

Bildung: Present Tense (progressive)		
am / are / is + Infinitiv mit Endung *-ing*	I **am** / you **are** / he / she / it **is** we **are** / you **are** / they **are**	work**ing** on a new project.

Verwendung: Present Tense (progressive)	
- bei Handlungen im Augenblick des Sprechens - bei vorübergehenden Handlungen - bei (fest) geplanten Handlungen in der Zukunft - bei gefühlsbetonten Aussagen mit *always* (negativ besetzt)	- I am reading a manual at the moment. - I'm staying at the Royal Excelsior Hotel. - I'm meeting Ms Winter next week. - He is always complaining about his boss.

Past Tense (Vergangenheit)

Bildung: Past Simple	
ed-Endung bei regelmäßigen Verben	I work**ed** in Munich last year.
2. Form bei unregelmäßigen Verben *(1. meet / 2. met / 3. met)*	He **met** Mr Miller yesterday.

Verwendung: Past Simple		
bei Vorgängen, die in der Vergangenheit abgeschlossen wurden; oft mit Zeitangabe. Signalwörter u. a.: *yesterday, in (1990), two weeks ago, last year, last month, last week.*	I finished my studies	in 2008. 3 years ago. last week.

Present Perfect (Vollendete Gegenwart)

Bildung: Present Perfect (simple)		
have oder *has* + *ed*-Endung (bei regelmäßigen Verben)	I / you / we / they **have worked** He / she **has worked**	as a trainee.
	It **has worked** well for us.	
3. Form bei unregelmäßigen Verben *(1. see / 2. saw / 3. seen)*	I have **seen** the new car.	

Bildung: Present Perfect (progressive)		
have / has + *been* + Infinitiv mit *-ing*	I / you / we / they **have** He / she **has**	**been living** in Munich **for** 5 years.

Verwendung: Present Perfect (simple and progressive)	
– bei Handlungen in der Vergangenheit **ohne Zeitangabe** – bei noch andauernden Zeitbestimmungen – bei Handlungen, die in der Vergangenheit begonnen haben, aber noch nicht abgeschlossen sind, wobei *for* bei Zeiträumen *(two hours / three weeks)* und *since* bei Zeitpunkten *(2001 / January)* benutzt wird – Einige Verben werden in der Regel nicht in der Verlaufsform verwendet.	– I have written three letters. – We haven't had any complaints so far / today … – I have been living in Stuttgart **for** 20 years. – I have been living in Stuttgart **since** 1982. – I have **had** the car for five years. – I have **known** the company since 2010.

Future (Zukunft)

Bildung und Verwendung	
Shall / will drückt äußere Umstände aus.	Most of this year's teleworking jobs **will** be offered in autumn.
Will drückt die Bereitschaft oder Entschlossenheit aus, etwas zu tun, sowie Versprechungen.	I'**ll** do my best to get the job.
Will wird auch benutzt für eine spontane Entscheidung.	Wait a minute, I'**ll** help you!
Going to wird verwendet, um persönliche Planungen und Vorhaben auszudrücken.	I **am going to** apply for a job in teleworking. *(Ich habe vor …)*
Going to wird auch verwendet, wenn bereits Anzeichen dafür da sind, dass etwas eintreten wird.	Look at those clouds! It'**s going to** rain.
Present continuous wird verwendet um eine feste Vereinbarung (gewöhnlich mit Zeitangabe) mitzuteilen.	Jennifer is **meeting** her colleague this evening.
Present simple wird für die Zukuft verwendet in Verbindung mit Fahrplänen, Öffnungszeiten usw.	Jim's train **arrives** at 4.30 p.m. Our office **opens** at 9 o'clock tomorrow morning.

Comparison of adjectives (Steigerung des Adjektivs)

Bildung	
Einsilbige und zweisilbige Adjektive werden durch Anhängen von *-er* und *-est* (germanische Steigerung) gesteigert.	fast – faster – fastest
Aus *y* wird *i*.	easy – easier – easiest
Ein einzelner Endkonsonant wird nach einfachem betonten Vokal verdoppelt.	hot – hotter – hottest
Für die zweisilbigen gibt es keine eindeutigen Regeln. Gewöhnlich werden zweisilbige Adjektive, die auf *-y*, *-le*, *-er* oder *-ow* enden germanisch gesteigert, aber dies ist keine bindende Regel.	clever – cleverer – cleverest noble – nobler – noblest narrow – narrower – narrowest
Ebenfalls germanisch gesteigert werden zweisilbige Adjektive, wenn sie ihre Betonung auf der zweiten Silbe haben. Auch diese Regel ist nicht bindend. Daneben gibt es aber z. B. auch folgende Formen: *more / the most clever* oder *more / the most polite*.	polite – politer – politest sincere – sincerer – sincerest
Andere zweisilbige Adjektive werden in der Regel romanisch gesteigert.	nervous – more nervous – most nervous splendid – more splendid – most splendid
Alle drei- und mehrsilbigen Adjektive steigert man mit *more* und *the most* (romanische Steigerung).	expensive – more expensive – the most expensive beautiful – more beautiful – the most beautiful
Es gibt auch eine Reihe von unregelmäßigen Adjektiven.	good – better – the best bad – worse – the worst much / many – more – the most little – less – the least old – elder – the eldest (bei Familienangehörigen)

Verwendung	
Gleichheiten mit *as … as*	He is **as** skilful **as** I. (so geschickt / fachmännisch wie ich)
Komparative mit *than*	Mike is **less** helpful **than** Tim. (weniger … als)
Je … desto…	**The** more I work with this machine **the** better I like it.
Superlativ beim Vergleich von mehr als 2 Objekten	The new electric drill is **the most** expensive tool in the brochure.

Adverbs (Adverbien)

> Das Umstandswort (Adverb) dient zur näheren Beschreibung eines Eigenschaftswortes (Adjektives) oder eines Zeitwortes (Verbs).

Bildung

Von der Wortbildung her unterscheidet man zwei Arten von Adverbien:	
1. ursprüngliche und durch Zusammensetzung gebildete Adverbien	often, quite, here, soon always, already, yesterday
2. durch Ableitung gebildete Abverbien: Hier wird an das Adjektiv ein *-ly* angehängt.	clear**ly**, usual**ly**, quick**ly**, easi**ly**, bad**ly**
Manche Adjektive und Adverbien sind	
– gleichlautend oder	daily, weekly, monthly, yearly, early, fast
– unterschiedlich.	good – **well**
Die Steigerung des Adverbs ist der Steigerung des Adjektivs vergleichbar.	carefully – more carefully – most carefully fast – faster – the fastest
Unregelmäßige Formen der Steigerung	well – better – best badly – worse – worst
y wird zu *i*	happy + -ly = happily
stummes *e* fällt weg	true + -ly = truly
Verdoppelung des Endkonsonanten	beautiful + -ly = beautifully

Verwendung

Hier wird das Verb näher beschrieben.	The new machine **works well**.
Hier wird das Adjektiv *clear* näher beschrieben.	The small printer makes **remarkably clear** printouts.
Hier wird ein anderes Adverb *(quickly)* näher beschrieben.	Our new machine works **extremely quickly**.

Questions (Fragen)

Bildung: Alternative questions (Entscheidungsfragen)

Entscheidungsfragen, die mit ja oder nein beantwortet werden können, werden im Englischen immer mit einem Hilfsverb oder einer Form von *to do* eingeleitet.	**Do** you smoke? **Did** you see Mr Miller yesterday?
Erstes Hilfsverb steht vor dem Subjekt.	**Have** you met Mr Miller?

Verwendung: Alternative questions (Entscheidungsfragen)	
Does Sally speak French?	Yes, she **does**. / No, she **doesn't**.
Can these tools be used in milling as well as in turning?	Yes, they **can**. / No, they **can't**.
Is the lathe set properly for this job?	Yes, it **is**. / No, it **isn't**.
Did he meet the chief executive at the fair?	Yes, he **did**. / No, he **didn't**.
Will you finish this job by Friday?	Yes, I **will**. / No, I **won't**.

Bildung: Questions with interrogatives (Fragen mit Fragefürwörtern)	
Die Fragen werden mit dem Fragefürwort eingeleitet. Vor dem Subjekt steht die Form von *to do (do / does; did)*, nach dem Subjekt steht das Vollverb im Infinitiv.	**How** do you **go** to work? **What** does she **do**?
Wird nach dem Subjekt oder einem Teil des Subjekts gefragt *(who, what, which, whose)*, so wird die Form von 'to do' nicht verwendet.	**What** is his job?

Verwendung: Questions with interrogatives (Fragen mit Fragefürwörtern)	
Fragewort ist Subjekt.	Who operates this machine? Which tools do you need for this job?
Fragewort ist nicht Subjekt.	Who / Whom did he meet at the exhibition? Which tool have you chosen for this job?

Word order (Wortstellung)

Bildung	
Die Wortstellung folgt im englischen Aussagesatz der Regel S – P – O: *Subject [They] – Predicate [have repaired] – Object [the broken tools]*	They have repaired the broken tools.
Dies gilt auch im Nebensatz (im Deutschen steht ja im Nebensatz das Prädikat am Ende).	I was told that they had repaired the broken tools.
Zeitbestimmungen stehen in der Regel entweder am Anfang oder am Ende des Satzes.	Yesterday they repaired the broken tools. They repaired the broken tools a week ago.
Mehrere Umstandsbestimmungen folgen gewöhnlich folgender Reihenfolge: *Manner – Place – Time* (Art und Weise – Ort – Zeit)	The mechanic repaired the tools in the shop yesterday. The mechanic repaired the tools quite skilfully in the shop last night.
Adverbien der Häufigkeit *(frequency)* können auch vor dem Hauptverb stehen: *always, ever, never, often, regularly, generally, rarely, seldom, occasionally*. Diese Adverbien stehen aber nach dem Verb *to be*. Bei Hilfsverben stehen die Adverbien der Häufigkeit zwischen dem Hilfsverb und dem Vollverb, bzw. nach dem Hilfsverb.	The service people **always** come on time. The service people **never** come without calling ahead. The service people **usually** check the machine in May. They are **generally** very reliable. The machine has **sometimes** had problems. With old machines you can **never** tell.

Defining relative clauses (Notwendige Relativsätze)

> Ein Relativsatz ist notwendig, wenn die darin gegebene Information nötig ist, um deutlich zu machen, welche Person oder Sache gemeint ist.

Verwendung	
bei Personen *who* oder *that*	The man **who** / **that** is operating the CNC machine usually works at the training centre.
bei Sachen *which* oder *that*	The machine element **which** / **that** is moving the tool is the main spindle.
im Genitiv wird **whose** verwendet	Tom is an engineer **whose** skills are highly praised.
Das Relativpronomen als Satzobjekt kann weggelassen werden.	They called the technician (**who**) they saw standing at the milling machine. Sally read the operation plan (**which**) she had filled in this morning.

Non-defining relative clauses (Nicht notwendige Relativsätze)

> Ein Relativsatz ist nicht notwendig, wenn die darin gegebene Information nicht nötig ist, um deutlich zu machen, welche Person oder Sache gemeint ist.

Verwendung	
Ein Relativsatz ist nicht notwendig, wenn die darin enthaltene Information nicht nötig ist, um zu erkennen, welche Person oder Sache gemeint ist.	**Sally's friend**, who is a skilled worker, **is doing his final exams this summer**. **The machine**, which is DEG's latest model, **works perfectly**.
Relativpronomen als Satzobjekt	**The three German apprentices**, who Sally met at the training centre, **are in their last year of training**.

Reported speech (Indirekte Rede)

Die indirekte Rede wird benutzt, wenn berichtet wird oder wurde, was jemand sagt oder sagte, bzw. macht oder machte (**Aussage**), wenn jemandem gesagt wird oder wurde, was geschehen soll (**Aufforderung**), oder wenn gefragt wird oder wurde, was geschieht oder geschah (**Frage**).

Bildung / Verwendung	
Steht das Wort, welches die indirekte Rede einleitet, in der Gegenwart, so ändern sich die Zeitformen der direkten Rede nicht.	"We **are measuring** this machined component." → Sally explains that they are measuring the machined component.
Steht das Wort, welches die indirekte Rede einleitet, in der Vergangenheit, so ändern sich die Zeitformen der direkten Rede wie folgt. *Simple past* und *present perfect* werden zu *past perfect*.	Sally **explained that they were measuring** the machined component. "The trainee **forgot** to set the revolution speed." → The master **noticed that the trainee had forgotten** to check the revolution speed.
Will wird zu *would*.	"The drilling operation **will** have to be prepared by marking out and centring." → Oliver **remembered** that the drilling operation **would** have to be prepared by marking out and centring.
Pronomen werden angepasst.	"**I can't** find the measuring equipment." → **Sally told** me that she **couldn't find** the measuring equipment.
Orts- und Zeitbestimmungen werden angepasst.	"**We** are seeing the other students **tomorrow**." → Oliver **added** that **they** were seeing the other students **the next day**. "I programmed the CNC machine **two days ago**." → He said that he had programmed the CNC machine **two days earlier**.
Aufforderungen werden in der indirekten Rede im Infinitiv wiedergegeben.	"**Use** HSS twist drills to drill metal stock." → The instructor **advised** Sally **to use** HSS twist drills to drill metal stock.
Bei Fragen wird die Wortstellung wie im Aussagesatz verwendet, d.h. am Anfang steht das Fragewort, dann folgen Subjekt, Prädikat und Objekt.	"Why has Oliver used the impact drilling function?" → The master **wanted to know why Oliver had used** the impact drilling function. "When did you sharpen the drill?" → He asked **when he had sharpened** the drill.
Die Umschreibung mit 'to do' wird nur bei Verneinungen angewendet.	"Why **don't** you call the salesman?" → She **asked** Sally why she **didn't call** the salesman.

Appendix | Grammar overview

Passive voice (Passiv)

Bildung	
Form von *to be* + *ed*-Endung (wie bei *simple past*) bei regelmäßigen Verben Form von *to be* + 3. Form bei unregelmäßigen Verben (*1. take / 2. took / 3. taken*. Siehe Liste der unregelmäßigen Verben.)	The machine **is equipped** with an emergency stop. He **is taken** to hospital.

Aktiv: We / recharge / the batteries.
        Subjekt / Prädikat / Objekt

Passiv: The batteries / are recharged / (by us).
        Subjekt / Prädikat / Objekt (by-agent)

Formen	
Present Tense (Simple)	The goods are transported every day.
Present Tense (Progressive)	The goods are being transported at the moment.
Past Tense (Simple)	The goods were transported yesterday.
Past Tense (Progressive)	The goods were being transported when the truck crashed.
Future 1 (will)	The goods will be transported next Monday, I promise.
Future 1 (going to)	The goods are going to be transported next month.
Present Perfect	The goods have already been transported.
Past Perfect	The goods had been transported before the order arrived.

Verwendung	
Das Passiv wird hauptsächlich verwendet, wenn der Ausführende (*by-agent*) unwichtig oder unbekannt ist oder nicht genannt werden soll. Deshalb wird der *by-agent* nur bei besonderer Betonung genannt.	The batteries **are recharged** (**by us**) when they are empty. A few years ago the first cars **were equipped** with airbags (**by the manufacturers**).
Die Passivkonstruktion wird besonders bei technischen Beschreibungen, Anweisungen in Handbüchern usw. verwendet. Bei der Umwandlung von Aktiv in Passiv wird das Objekt des Aktivsatzes zum Subjekt des Passivsatzes.	Aktiv: We recharge **the batteries**. Passiv: **The batteries** are recharged (by us).
Im Gegensatz zum Deutschen können bestimmte Verben im Englischen im Passiv verwendet werden. Die Übersetzung ins Deutsche erfolgt durch eine Konstruktion mit 'man'.	The fuel cell is considered to be a very promising invention. *(Man hält die Brennstoffzelle für eine sehr zukunftsweisende Erfindung.)*
Die Verlaufsform ist im Passiv nur im *Present Tense* und *Past Tense* gebräuchlich.	He **is being** taken to hospital. *(Er wird gerade ins Krankenhaus gebracht.)* He **was being** taken to hospital. *(Er wurde gerade ins Krankenhaus gebracht.)*

Gerund (Gerundium)

Wie im Deutschen kann man auch im Englischen aus einem Verb ein Substantiv machen. Beispiel: Durch häufiges **Messen** können Fehler vermieden werden.

Bildung		
Anhängen von *-ing* an den Infinitiv (Grundform) des Verbs	check + ing = checking drill + ing = drilling	
Verdoppelung eines Endkonsonanten (Mitlaut) nach einem Vokal (Selbstlaut)	put – putting control – controlling	travel – travelling refuel – refuelling
Stummes *e* fällt weg: aber: *agree – agreeing; see – seeing*	file – filing measure – measuring	

Verwendung	
Ein *gerund* kann Subjekt (Satzgegenstand) sein. Ebenso kann es die Funktion eines Objekts (Satzergänzung) haben.	**Filing** is rarely done by hand. He began **cleaning** the machine.
Nach Präpositionen (Verhältniswörtern) oder präpositionalen Ausdrücken steht ebenfalls das *gerund*.	He was afraid **of setting** the lever to a higher speed. They objected **to trying** the new software **without having** made a backup of the hard drive. The manager apologised **for being** late. They prevented the visitors **from entering** the production area without a hard hat. He was tired **of hearing** the same complaint.
Nach bestimmten Verben (Zeitwörtern) steht das *gerund*.	Try to **avoid overheating** the machine. The trainer **recommended turning** the machine off. We cannot **risk losing** this customer. Phillip **suggested using** a different production method.
Weitere Verben, die ein *gerund* nach sich haben.	enjoy, like, dislike, remember, stop He enjoys working in Italy.

Prepositions (Verhältniswörter)

Präpositionen geben das Verhältnis von Personen oder Dingen zueinander an (z. B. räumlich oder zeitlich).

Räumliche Präpositionen			
above	oberhalb	**into**	in … hinein
across	durch, quer durch	**off**	von … herunter, von … weg
at	neben, bei	**on, upon**	auf
opposite	gegenüber		

Räumliche Präpositionen

behind	hinter	**out, out of**	aus, heraus
below	unter, unterhalb	**through**	durch
beneath	unter, unterhalb	**to**	zu, nach, in Richtung auf
beside	neben	**towards**	auf … zu (Richtung)
between	zwischen	**under**	unter
in	in	**within**	innerhalb

Zeitliche Präpositionen

at	an, in	**from**	von
before	vor	**in**	am, im (Jahre)
between	zwischen	**on**	an, am
by	bis, bis spätestens	**since**	seit (Zeitpunkt)
during	während	**until, till**	bis
for	seit (Zeitraum)		

Modale Präpositionen und Präpositionen des Grundes

according to	entsprechend, gemäß	**despite, in spite of**	trotz
because of	wegen	**with**	mit
besides	außer	**without**	ohne

Verwendung

Laut Gebrauchsanweisung sollte **das Auswechseln** der Werkzeuge kein Problem darstellen.	**According to** the manual, there should be no problem **with** changing the tools.
… **hinten** im Raum	The machine is **at** the back of the room.
… **unten** auf jeder Seite	You'll find the number of the module **at** the bottom of every page.
… **am** Eingang	They were waiting **at** the entrance when it happened.
… ist **gegenüber / auf der anderen Seite**	The printer is **across** the hall.
… rannte quer **über** die Straße	The dog ran **across** the road.
… **zwischen** zwei Aktenmappen (räumlich)	He found the letter **between** two folders.
… **zwischen** 9 und 10 Uhr (zeitlich)	Why don't we meet **between** nine and ten?
… nur **während**	Smoking is allowed **during** the lunch break only!
… **von** … **bis**	He worked in Cardiff **from** December **until** January.
… **auf** der Straße	You should not park your car **in** the street.
… **bis** (spätestens)	You must be back **by** six o'clock at the latest.

Modal auxiliaries (Modale Hilfsverben)

> Die modalen Hilfsverben werden im Englischen oft auch *defective* (d.h. unvollständige) *auxiliaries* genannt, denn sie können in der Regel nur das Präsens bilden. Für die übrigen Zeiten müssen Ersatzformen verwendet werden.

Bildung		
Hilfsverb	**Ersatzform**	**deutsche Bedeutung**
can	to be able to	können, fähig sein, in der Lage sein
can	to be allowed to	dürfen, die Erlaubnis haben
may	to be allowed to	dürfen, die Erlaubnis haben
must	to have to	müssen
mustn't	not to be allowed to	nicht dürfen
needn't	not to have to	nicht brauchen, nicht müssen

Verwendung	
Present Tense: You **must** read the installation instructions very carefully.	**Simple past:** Yesterday he **had to** read the installation instructions twice because they were badly translated.
After the installation is completed you **needn't reboot** your system.	I **didn't have to** reboot my system when I installed the screensaver the other day.
Present Tense: He **can** handle software problems quite well.	**Present perfect:** Up to now he **has been able** to handle software problems quite well.
Present Tense: You **must not smoke** in the office.	**Future:** You **will not be allowed** to smoke in the office.

Participles (Partizipien)

Bildung	
Present Participle Infinitiv + *-ing*	Wind turbines are a **promising** option.
Past Participle 3. Stammform: *damaged* (*ed*-Endung wie bei *simple past*); (3. Form bei unregelmäßigen Verben: *1. know / 2. knew / 3. known*. Siehe Liste der unregelmäßigen Verben.)	After the storm we had to replace three **damaged** solar panels.

Verwendung	
als Adjektiv	It is a **known** fact that solar power can be used as an alternative energy.
Partizipialkonstruktionen dienen zur **Verkürzung** von: 1. adverbialen Nebensätzen mit Konjunktion *(when, although, as, while,...)* 2. adverbialen Nebensätzen ohne Konjunktion 3. Relativsätzen	 When **planning** to build a home, you should consider using solar energy to heat your water. **Unlocking** the warehouse door, he smelled gas. Wind farms **built** along the coast are most efficient.
Partizipialkonstruktionen zur **Verknüpfung** von zwei Hauptsätzen.	The guide led us through the factory. He warned us to stay away from the machines. The guide led us through the factory **warning** us to stay away from the machines.

If-clauses (Bedingungssätze)

> Man unterscheidet drei Arten von Bedingungen:
> 1. erfüllbare Bedingungen
> 2. Bedingungen, deren Erfüllung unwahrscheinlich ist
> 3. Bedingungen, die überhaupt nicht mehr erfüllt werden können.
>
> Zusätzlich zu den drei Typen gibt es noch einen weiteren Typ, der Regeln und Naturgesetze ausdrückt.

Bildung und Verwendung	
Type I (probable condition)	If you **lubricate** this machine regularly, it **will run** smoothly for a long time. *(Wenn man die Maschine regelmäßig ölt, läuft sie lange Zeit problemlos.)*
Type II (improbable condition)	If you **lubricated** this machine regularly, **it would** run smoothly for a long time. *(Wenn man diese Maschine regelmäßig ölen würde, würde sie für lange Zeit problemlos laufen.)*
Type III (impossible condition)	If you **had lubricated** this machine regularly, it **would have run** smoothly for a long time. *(Wenn man die Maschine regelmäßig geölt hätte, wäre sie lange Zeit problemlos gelaufen (jetzt läuft sie aber offensichtlich nicht mehr).*
Rules and laws of nature Hier handelt es sich im eigentlichen Sinne nicht mehr um eine Bedingung, sondern um ein Naturgesetz. Deshalb steht im Hauptsatz auch kein Futur, sondern ebenfalls das Präsens.	If you **heat** ice, it **melts**. *(Wenn man Eis erhitzt, schmilzt es.)*
Besonderheit bei Formen von *to be*	If I **were** you, I wouldn't use a combination spanner here.

Chronological word list

🌐 Videotraining: Englische Aussprache

Perfekte englische Aussprache leicht gemacht: Mit dem Lernprogramm zur englischen Lautschrift können Sie alle Laute einüben. Wählen Sie einfach in der Navigation rechts den entsprechenden Reiter (*Vowels* oder *Consonants*) aus und klicken Sie dann auf das gewünschte phonetische Symbol. Sprechen Sie die Wörter laut nach.

Unter www.klett.de geben Sie bitte den Code unter der Abbildung rechts ein.

🌐 n633sn

Abkürzungen und Zeichen

etw. = etwas	sth. = something
Pl. = Plural	BE = britisches Englisch
jmdn., jmdm. = jemanden, jemandem	AE = amerikanisches Englisch
sb. = somebody	⊙ = Vokabeln zu den Hörtexten

Module 1 Meeting people

confident [ˈkɒnfɪdənt] sicher, selbstbewusst
appropriate [əˈprəʊpriət] angemessen, passend

A | Saying "hello" and "goodbye" and giving your name

existing [ɪgˈzɪstɪŋ] bestehend
trade fair [ˈtreɪd ˌfeə] Messe
job fair [ˈdʒɒb ˌfeə] Jobmesse

B | Intercultural awareness

politeness [pəˈlaɪtnəs] Höflichkeit
pleasantry [ˈplezntri] höfliche Floskel
profitability [ˌprɒfɪtəˈbɪləti] Rentabilität
to chat [tʃæt] sich unterhalten
health [helθ] Gesundheit
pleasant [ˈpleznt] angenehm
to waste time [ˌweɪst ˈtaɪm] Zeit verschwenden
impression [ɪmˈpreʃn] Eindruck

conference [ˈkɒnfrəns] Tagung
minutes [ˈmɪnɪts] Protokoll
polite [pəˈlaɪt] höflich
usual [ˈjuːʒl] gewöhnlich, üblich, normal
upset [ʌpˈset] verärgert
stranger [ˈstreɪndʒə] Unbekannte(r)
on the other hand [ɒn ði ˌʌðə ˈhænd] andererseits
in charge of [ɪn ˈtʃɑːdʒ əv] verantwortlich für
cash register [ˈkæʃ ˌredʒɪstə] Kasse
given name [ˌgɪvn ˈneɪm] Vorname
family name [ˌfæmli ˈneɪm] Nachname
to intend [ɪnˈtend] beabsichtigen

Module 2 Your company

regardless of [rɪˈgɑːdləs ˌəv] ungeachtet, unabhängig von
furniture [ˈfɜːnɪtʃə] Möbel
likely [ˈlaɪkli] wahrscheinlich
supplier [səˈplaɪə] Lieferant

Appendix | Chronological word list

skill [skɪl] Fähigkeit, Fertigkeit
to express [ɪkˈspres] zum Ausdruck bringen
tool [tuːl] Werkzeug

B | The company and its departments

department [dɪˈpɑːtmənt] Abteilung
to distribute [dɪˈstrɪbjuːt] vertreiben, verteilen
damaged [ˈdæmɪdʒd] beschädigt
employee [ɪmˈplɔɪiː] Beschäftigte(r), Angestellte(r)
accounts [əˈkaʊnts] Buchhaltung
raw materials [ˌrɔː məˈtɪəriəlz] Rohstoffe
human resources [ˌhjuːmən ˈriːzɔːsɪz] Personalabteilung
to recruit [rɪˈkruːt] rekrutieren, anstellen
purchasing (department) [ˈpɜːtʃəsɪŋ (dɪˌpɑːtmənt)] Einkauf(-sabteilung)
to maintain [meɪnˈteɪn] warten, in Stand halten
R&D (Research and Development) [rɪˌsɜːtʃ ən dɪˈveləpmənt] Forschungs- und Entwicklungsabteilung
to develop [dɪˈveləp] entwickeln
in charge of [ɪn ˈtʃɑːdʒ əv] zuständig für

◉ **to cover** [ˈkʌvə] abdecken, bedecken
headquarters [ˌhedˈkwɔːtəz] Hauptsitz
to found [faʊnd] gründen
family-owned [ˈfæmliˈəʊnd] in Familienbesitz
manufacturing plant [ˌmænjəˈfæktʃərɪŋ ˌplɑːnt] Produktionsbetrieb
currently [ˈkʌrəntli] derzeit, zurzeit, momentan
braking system [ˈbreɪkɪŋ ˌsɪstəm] Bremsanlage
internship (AE) [ˈɪntɜːrnʃɪp] Praktikum
device [dɪˈvaɪs] Gerät
cylinder head [ˈsɪlɪndə ˌhed] Zylinderkopf
to inspect [ɪnˈspekt] prüfen
operating system [ˈɒpreɪtɪŋ ˌsɪstəm] Betriebssystem
interface [ˈɪntəfeɪs] Schnittstelle, Interface

B | Tasks and responsibilities

task [tɑːsk] Aufgabe
responsibility [rɪˌspɒnsəˈbɪləti] Verantwortung
to manufacture [ˌmænjəˈfæktʃə] herstellen
to occur [əˈkɜː] vorkommen
apprenticeship [əˈprentɪsʃɪp] Ausbildung, Lehre
branch [brɑːnʃ] Niederlassung
precision [prɪˈsɪʒn] Genauigkeit
essential [ɪˈsenʃl] wesentlich, unbedingt erforderlich

to drill [drɪl] bohren
to shape [ʃeɪp] formen, fräsen
to polish [ˈpɒlɪʃ] abschleifen, polieren
to intervene [ˌɪntəˈviːn] einschreiten
to vibrate [vaɪˈbreɪt] vibrieren
workpiece [ˈwɜːkpiːs] Werkstück
to monitor [ˈmɒnɪtə] überwachen, kontrollieren, beobachten
to measure [ˈmeʒə] messen
dimension [daɪˈmenʃn] Maß, Abmessung
lubricated [ˈluːbrɪkeɪtɪd] geölt
lubricating oil [ˈluːbrɪkeɪtɪŋ ˌɔɪl] Schmieröl
generally [ˈdʒenrəli] normalerweise, im Allgemeinen
shift [ʃɪft] Schicht
to prefer [prɪˈfɜː] bevorzugen
rarely [ˈreəli] selten
accuracy [ˈækjərəsi] Genauigkeit
to include [ɪnˈkluːd] einbeziehen, einschließen
to swap [swɒp] tauschen

C | Organisational structure

to employ [ɪmˈplɔɪ] beschäftigen
to support [səˈpɔːt] unterstützen
to split [splɪt] aufteilen
core area [ˌkɔː ˈeəriə] Kernbereich
to report to [rɪˈpɔːt tuː] unterstehen
to belong to [bɪˈlɒŋ tuː] gehören zu
experienced [ɪkˈspɪəriənst] erfahren
capable [ˈkeɪpəbl] fähig
closely [ˈkləʊsli] eng

Module 3 Telephoning

line [laɪn] (hier:) Branche
to fix [fɪks] reparieren
leak [liːk] undichte Stelle
to install [ɪnˈstɔːl] installieren, montieren, anschließen
complaint [kəmˈpleɪnt] Beschwerde, Reklamation
order [ˈɔːdə] Bestellung, Auftrag
necessary [ˈnesəsri] nötig, notwendig
delay [dɪˈleɪ] Verspätung, Verzögerung
breakdown [ˈbreɪkdaʊn] Panne, Störung
solution [səˈluːʃn] Lösung
confused [kənˈfjuːzd] verwirrt
crash [kræʃ] Absturz

A | Making and receiving a phone call

meeting [ˈmiːtɪŋ] Sitzung, Besprechung
country code [ˈkʌntri ˌkəʊd] Ländervorwahl
area code [ˈeərɪə ˌkəʊd] Vorwahl
extension number [ɪkˈstenʃn ˌnʌmbə] Durchwahl
suitable [ˈsuːtəbl] geeignet, passend
polite [pəˈlaɪt] höflich
although [ɔːlˈðəʊ] obwohl
to remain [rɪˈmeɪn] bleiben
request [rɪˈkwest] Bitte
grateful [ˈɡreɪtfl] dankbar
whereas [weəˈræz] während
impolite [ˌɪmpəˈlaɪt] unhöflich

B | Giving information over the phone

valuable [ˈvæljuəbl] *(hier:)* wichtig
figures [ˈfɪɡəz] Nummern, Daten
clearly [ˈklɪəli] deutlich, klar

> **confused** [kənˈfjuːzd] verwirrt
> **to divert** [daɪˈvɜːrt] weiterleiten
> **extractor fan** [ɪkˈstræktə fæn] Dunstabzug
> **hob** [hɒb] Kochfeld
> **diameter** [daɪˈæmətə] Durchmesser
> **socket** [ˈsɒkɪt] Steckdose

Module 4 Written communication

essential [ɪˈsenʃl] sehr wichtig
workshop [ˈwɜːkʃɒp] Werkstatt
efficiently [ɪˈfɪʃntli] effizient
necessary [ˈnesəsri] nötig, notwendig
enquiry [ɪnˈkwaɪəri] Anfrage
promptly [ˈprɒmtli] sofort
offer [ˈɒfə] Angebot
order [ˈɔːdə] Bestellung
to replace [rɪˈpleɪs] ersetzen
lesser [ˈlesə] geringer
advantage [ədˈvɑːntɪdʒ] Vorteil
disadvantage [ˌdɪsədˈvɑːntɪdʒ] Nachteil
confidential [ˌkɒnfɪˈdenʃl] vertraulich
time-consuming [ˈtaɪmkənˌsjuːmɪŋ] zeitraubend
reliable [rɪˈlaɪəbl] zuverlässig
misunderstanding [ˌmɪsʌndəˈstændɪŋ] Missverständnis

A | Enquiries

enquiry [ɪnˈkwaɪəri] Anfrage
appropriate [əˈprəʊpriət] angemessen, passend
salutation [ˌsæljəˈteɪʃn] (Brief:) Anrede
supplier [səˈplaɪə] Lieferant, Zulieferer
subject line [ˈsʌbdʒɪkt ˌlaɪn] (Brief:) Betreffzeile
family-run [ˌfæmliˈrʌn] in Familienbesitz, familiengeführt
catalogue [ˈkætəlɒɡ] Katalog
discount [ˈdɪskaʊnt] Rabatt, Preisnachlass
terms of payment [ˌtɜːmz əv ˈpeɪmənt] Zahlungsbedingungen
delivery times [dɪˈlɪvri ˌtaɪmz] Lieferzeiten
closing phrase [ˈkləʊzɪŋ ˌfreɪz] Schlussworte
complimentary close [ˌkɒmplɪmentri ˈkləʊz] Grußformel (am Briefende)
to recommend [ˌrekəˈmend] empfehlen
cost estimate [ˈkɒst ˌestɪmət] Kostenvoranschlag
to appreciate [əˈpriːʃieɪt] (wert-)schätzen
supply from stock [səˌplaɪ frəm ˈstɒk] ab Lager liefern

B | Offers

bank transfer [ˈbæŋk ˌtrænsfɜː] Banküberweisung
working day [ˌwɜːkɪŋ ˈdeɪ] Werktag
attachment [əˈtætʃmənt] Anhang
stock [stɒk] Bestand, Vorrat
to require [rɪˈkwaɪə] benötigen
DIY (Do-it-yourself) [ˌdiːaɪˈwaɪ] Heimwerken
sum [sʌm] Betrag
consignment [kənˈsaɪnmənt] Lieferung, Sendung

Module 5 Applications

application [ˌæplɪˈkeɪʃn] Bewerbung
branch [brɑːnʃ] Niederlassung
advert [ˈædvɜːt] Anzeige
letter of application [ˌletər əv ˌæplɪˈkeɪʃn] Bewerbungsschreiben
CV (curriculum vitae) [ˌsiːˈviː, kəˌrɪkjələm ˈviːtaɪ] Lebenslauf
job interview [ˈdʒɒb ˌɪntəvjuː] Vorstellungsgespräch
employment contract [ɪmˈplɔɪmənt ˌkɒntrækt] Arbeitsvertrag
to invite [ɪnˈvaɪt] einladen
skill [skɪl] Fähigkeit
industry [ˈɪndəstri] *(hier:)* Branche
hard-working [ˌhɑːdˈwɜːkɪŋ] fleißig

Appendix | Chronological word list

A | Job advertisements

recently [ˈriːsntli] kürzlich
willing to learn [ˌwɪlɪŋ tə ˈlɜːn] lernbereit, lernwillig
responsible [rɪˈspɒnsəbl] verantwortlich
punctual [ˈpʌŋktʃuəl] pünktlich
pleasant [ˈpleznt] angenehm, sympathisch
working atmosphere [ˌwɜːkɪŋ ˈætməsfɪə] Arbeitsklima
valid [ˈvælɪd] gültig
summary [ˈsʌmri] Zusammenfassung

B | Letter of application

letter of application [ˌletər əv ˌæplɪˈkeɪʃn] Bewerbungsschreiben
to decide [dɪˈsaɪd] sich entscheiden
internship (AE) [ˈɪntɜːnʃɪp] Praktikum
opportunity [ˌɒpəˈtjuːnəti] Möglichkeit
theoretical [θɪəˈretɪkl] theoretisch
to gain [ɡeɪn] (hier:) sammeln
reliable [rɪˈlaɪəbl] zuverlässig
to consider [kənˈsɪdə] betrachten
to require [rɪˈkwaɪə] benötigen

C | The CV

advice [ədˈvaɪs] Rat
tip [tɪp] Tipp, Hinweis
to highlight [ˈhaɪlaɪt] betonen
strength [streŋθ] Stärke
achievement [əˈtʃiːvmənt] Leistung
supervisor [ˈsuːpəvaɪzə] Leiter(in), Kontrolleur(in)
truth [truːθ] Wahrheit
embarrassing [ɪmˈbærəsɪŋ] peinlich
to spell [spel] buchstabieren
grateful [ˈɡreɪtfl] dankbar

Module 6 Socialising

relationship [rɪˈleɪʃnʃɪp] Beziehung

A | Small talk

subsidiary [səbˈsɪdiəri] Tochtergesellschaft
trainee [ˌtreɪˈniː] Auszubildende(r)
appropriate [əˈprəʊpriət] angemessen, passend

B | Small talk in business

to dismiss [dɪˈsmɪs] nicht beachten
common ground [ˌkɒmən ˈɡraʊnd] gemeinsame Basis
trivial [ˈtrɪviəl] unwichtig
uneasiness [ʌnˈiːzinəs] Unbehagen
tension [ˈtenʃn] Spannung
to avoid [əˈvɔɪd] vermeiden
awkward [ˈɔːkwəd] peinlich, unangenehm

C | Eating out

well-done [ˌwelˈdʌn] (Steak) gut durchgebraten
pork [pɔːk] Schweinefleisch
side order [ˈsaɪd ˌɔːdə] Beilage
bill [bɪl] Rechnung
game [ɡeɪm] (hier:) Wild
dessert [dɪˈzɜːt] Nachtisch, Nachspeise
fork [fɔːk] Gabel
main dish [ˌmeɪn ˈdɪʃ] Hauptgericht
beef [biːf] Rindfleisch
poultry [ˈpəʊltri] Geflügel
starter [ˈstɑːtə] Vorspeise
tip [tɪp] Trinkgeld

Module 7 Presentations

required [rɪˈkwaɪəd] erforderlich, verlangt, erwünscht
service [ˈsɜːvɪs] Dienstleistung
to develop [dɪˈveləp] entwickeln
to improve [ɪmˈpruːv] besser werden, sich verbessern
meeting [ˈmiːtɪŋ] Sitzung, Besprechung
graph [ɡrɑːf] Diagramm
chart [tʃɑːt] Schaubild, Diagramm
preparation [ˌprepəˈreɪʃn] Vorbereitung
to explain [ɪkˈspleɪn] erklären
sales pitch [ˈseɪlz ˌpɪtʃ] Verkaufspräsentation
reason [ˈriːzn] Grund

A | Preparing a presentation

audience [ˈɔːdiəns] Zuhörer (Pl.), Publikum
body language [ˈbɒdi ˌlæŋɡwɪdʒ] Körpersprache
handout [ˈhændaʊt] Informationsblatt
to prepare [prɪˈpeə] vorbereiten
visual aids [ˌvɪʒuəl ˈeɪdz] Anschauungsmaterial, visuelle Hilfen

to describe [dɪˈskraɪb] beschreiben
summary [ˈsʌmri] Zusammenfassung
overview [ˈəʊvəvjuː] Überblick
to reinforce [ˌriːɪnˈfɔːs] verstärken, betonen
guidelines [ˈgaɪdlaɪnz] Leitlinien

B | Describing materials and products

sturdy [ˈstɜːdi] robust
shiny [ˈʃaɪni] glänzend
robust [rəˈbʌst] stabil
state-of-the-art [ˌsteɪt əv ðiˈ ɑːt] auf dem neuesten Stand (der Technik)
user-friendly [ˌjuːzəˈfrendli] benutzerfreundlich
reliable [rɪˈlaɪəbl] zuverlässig
hand-crafted [ˌhænˈkrɑːftɪd] handgefertigt

C | Delivering a presentation

carpenter [ˈkɑːpɪntə] Tischler(in), Zimmerer, Zimmerin
furniture [ˈfɜːnɪtʃə] Möbel
trade show [ˈtreɪd ʃəʊ] Messe
lounger [ˈlaʊndʒə] Liegesessel
convenience [kənˈviːniəns] Zweckmäßigkeit, Bequemlichkeit

---

durable [ˈdjʊərəbl] haltbar
joiner [ˈdʒɔɪnə] Tischler(in), Schreiner(in)
polyurethane coating [ˌpɒlɪjʊərəθeɪn ˈkəʊtɪŋ] Polyurethanbeschichtung
softwood [ˈsɒftˌwʊd] Weichholz
timber [ˈtɪmbə] Holz, Bauholz
varnish [ˈvɑːnɪʃ] Lack

Module 8 Dealing with customers

to deal with [ˈdiːl wɪð] umgehen mit, sich befassen mit
customer [ˈkʌstəmə] Kunde, Kundin
success [səkˈses] Erfolg
appointment [əˈpɔɪntmənt] Termin
enquiry [ɪnˈkwaɪəri] Anfrage
complaint [kəmˈpleɪnt] Beschwerde
essential [ɪˈsenʃl] sehr wichtig

A | Complaints

solution [səˈluːʃn] Lösung
delay [dɪˈleɪ] Verzögerung, Verspätung
price reduction [ˈpraɪs rɪˌdʌkʃn] Preisnachlass
faulty [ˈfɒlti] fehlerhaft, defekt, mangelhaft
damaged [ˈdæmɪdʒd] beschädigt
unsatisfactory [ʌnˌsætɪsˈfæktri] unbefriedigend, ungenügend, unzureichend
to replace [rɪˈpleɪs] ersetzen
air freight [ˈeə ˌfreɪt] Luftfracht
surplus [ˈsɜːpləs] überschüssig
credit note [ˈkredɪt ˌnəʊt] Gutschrift
specific [spəˈsɪfɪk] bestimmt, spezifisch
access [ˈækses] Zugang
to log on [ˌlɒg ˈɒn] sich anmelden, sich einwählen
migration [maɪˈgreɪʃn] (hier:) Umstellung
redo [ˌriːˈduː] noch einmal machen
to look into sth. [ˌlʊk ˈɪntə] einer Sache nachgehen
technician [tekˈnɪʃn] Techniker(in)
plumbing and heating [ˌplʌmɪŋ ənd ˈhiːtɪŋ] Heizung und Sanitär

B | Customer service

upset [ʌpˈset] verärgert
to avoid [əˈvɔɪd] vermeiden
argument [ˈɑːgjəmənt] Streit, Auseinandersetzung
to calm sb. [kɑːm] jmdn. beruhigen
to reassure [ˌriːəˈʃʊə] beruhigen
patient [ˈpeɪʃnt] geduldig
to solve [sɒlv] lösen
frame of mind [ˌfreɪm əv ˈmaɪnd] geistige Verfassung
furious [ˈfjʊəriəs] wütend
to affect [əˈfekt] Einfluss nehmen auf
mood [muːd] Laune
to blame sb. / sth. for sth. [bleɪm] jmdm. / etw. die Schuld an etw. geben, jmdn. verantwortlich machen
excuse [ɪkˈskjuːs] Ausrede

Alphabetical word list

A

access Zugang 37
accounts Buchhaltung 13
accuracy Genauigkeit 15
achievement Leistung 27
advantage Vorteil 20
advert Anzeige 24
advice Rat 27
to affect Einfluss nehmen auf 39
air freight Luftfracht 37
although obwohl 18
application Bewerbung 24
appointment Termin 36
to appreciate (wert-)schätzen 21
apprenticeship Ausbildung, Lehre 14
appropriate angemessen, passend 8
area code Vorwahl 17
argument Streit, 39
attachment Anhang 22
audience Zuhörer (Pl.), Publikum 33
to avoid vermeiden 39
awkward peinlich, unangenehm 30

B

bank transfer Banküberweisung 22
beef Rindfleisch 31
to belong to gehören zu 15
bill Rechnung 31
to blame sb./sth. for sth. jmdm./etw. die Schuld an etw. geben, jmdn. verantwortlich machen 39
body language Körpersprache 33
braking system Bremsanlage 13
branch Niederlassung 24
breakdown Panne, Störung 16

C

to calm sb. jmdn. beruhigen 39
capable fähig 15
carpenter Tischler(in), Zimmerer, Zimmerin 35
cash register Kasse 11
catalogue Katalog 21

chart Schaubild, Diagramm 32
to chat sich unterhalten 11
clearly deutlich, klar 19
closely eng 15
closing phrase Schlussworte 21
common ground gemeinsame Basis 30
complaint Beschwerde 36
complimentary close Grußformel (am Briefende) 21
conference Tagung 11
confident sicher, selbstbewusst 8
confidential vertraulich 20
configure konfigurieren 21
confused verwirrt 16
to consider betrachten 26
consignment Lieferung, Sendung 23
convenience Zweckmäßigkeit, Bequemlichkeit 35
core area Kernbereich 15
cost estimate Kostenvoranschlag 21
country code Ländervorwahl 17
to cover abdecken, bedecken 13
crash Absturz 16
credit note Gutschrift 37
currently derzeit, zurzeit, momentan 13
customer Kunde, Kundin 36
CV (curriculum vitae) Lebenslauf 24
cylinder head Zylinderkopf 13

D

damaged beschädigt 13
to deal with umgehen mit, sich befassen mit 36
to decide sich entscheiden 24
delay Verspätung, Verzögerung 16
delivery times Lieferzeiten 21
department Abteilung 13
to describe beschreiben 33
dessert Nachtisch, Nachspeise 31
to develop entwickeln 32
device Gerät 13
diameter Durchmesser 19

dimension Maß, Abmessung 14
disadvantage Nachteil 20
discount Rabatt, Preisnachlass 21
to dismiss nicht beachten 30
to distribute vertreiben, verteilen 13
to divert weiterleiten 19
DIY (Do-it-yourself) Heimwerken 22
to drill bohren 14
durable haltbar 35

E

efficiently effizient 20
embarrassing peinlich 27
to employ beschäftigen 15
employee Beschäftigte(r), Angestellte(r) 13
employment contract Arbeitsvertrag 24
enquiry Anfrage 36
essential sehr wichtig 36
excuse Ausrede 39
existing bestehend 9
experienced erfahren 15
to explain erklären 32
to express zum Ausdruck bringen 12
extension number Durchwahl 17
extractor fan Dunstabzugshaube 19

F

family name Nachname 11
family-owned in Familienbesitz 13
family-run in Familienbesitz, familiengeführt 21
faulty fehlerhaft, defekt, mangelhaft 37
figures Nummern, Daten 19
to fix reparieren 16
fork Gabel 31
to found gründen 13
frame of mind geistige Verfassung 39
furious wütend 39
furniture Möbel 12

G

to gain (*hier:*) sammeln 26
game (*hier:*) Wild 31
generally normalerweise, im Allgemeinen 14
given name Vorname 11
graph Diagramm 32
grateful dankbar 18
guidelines Leitlinien 33

H

hand-crafted handgefertigt 34
handout Informationsblatt 33
hard-working fleißig 24
headquarters Hauptsitz 13
health Gesundheit 11
to highlight betonen 27
hob Kochfeld 19
human resources Personalabteilung 13

I

impolite unhöflich 18
impression Eindruck 11
to improve besser werden, sich verbessern 32
in charge of verantwortlich für 11
to include einbeziehen, einschließen 15
industry (*hier:*) Branche 24
to inspect prüfen 13
to install installieren, montieren, anschließen 16
to intend beabsichtigen 11
interface Schnittstelle, Interface 13
internship Praktikum 13
to intervene einschreiten 14
to invite einladen 24

J

job fair Jobmesse 9
job interview Vorstellungsgespräch 24
joiner Tischler(in), Schreiner(in) 35

L

leak undichte Stelle 16
lesser geringer 20
letter of application Bewerbungsschreiben 26
likely wahrscheinlich 12
line (*hier:*) Branche 16
to log on sich anmelden, sich einwählen 37
to look into sth. einer Sache nachgehen 37
lounger Liegesessel 35
lubricated geölt 14
lubricating oil Schmieröl 14

M

main dish Hauptgericht 31
to maintain warten, in Stand halten 13
to manufacture herstellen 14
manufacturing plant Produktionsbetrieb 13
to measure messen 14
meeting Sitzung, Besprechung 32
migration (*hier:*) Umstellung 37
minutes Protokoll 11
misunderstanding Missverständnis 20
to monitor überwachen, kontrollieren, beobachten 14
mood Laune 39

N

necessary nötig, notwendig 20

O

to occur vorkommen 14
offer Angebot 20
on the other hand andererseits 11
operating system Betriebssystem 13
opportunity Möglichkeit 24
order Bestellung 20
overview Überblick 33

P

patient geduldig 39
pleasant angenehm 11
pleasantry höfliche Floskel 11
plumbing and heating Heizung und Sanitär 38
to polish abschleifen, polieren 14
polite höflich 11
politeness Höflichkeit 11
polyurethane coating Polyurethanbeschichtung 35
pork Schweinefleisch 31
poultry Geflügel 31
precision Genauigkeit 14
to prefer bevorzugen 14
preparation Vorbereitung 32
to prepare vorbereiten 33
price reduction Preisnachlass 37
profitability Rentabilität 11
promptly sofort 20
punctual pünktlich 25
purchasing (department) Einkauf (-sabteilung) 13

R

rarely selten 15
raw materials Rohstoffe 13
R&D (Research and Development) Forschungs- und Entwicklungsabteilung 13
reason Grund 32
to reassure beruhigen 39
recently kürzlich 25
to recommend empfehlen 21
to recruit rekrutieren, anstellen 13
redo noch einmal machen 37
regardless of ungeachtet, unabhängig von 12
to reinforce verstärken, betonen 33
relationship Beziehung 28
reliable zuverlässig 20
to remain bleiben 18
to replace ersetzen 20
to report to unterstehen 15
request Bitte 18
to require benötigen 22
required erforderlich, verlangt, erwünscht 32
responsibility Verantwortung 14
responsible verantwortlich 25
robust stabil 34

S

sales pitch Verkaufspräsentation 32
salutation (Brief:) Anrede 21
service Dienstleistung 32
to shape formen, fräsen 14

Appendix | Alphabetical word list

shift Schicht 14
shiny glänzend 34
side order Beilage 31
skill Fähigkeit 24
socket Steckdose 19
softwood Weichholz 35
solution Lösung 16
to solve lösen 39
specific bestimmt, spezifisch 37
to spell buchstabieren 27
to split aufteilen 15
starter Vorspeise 31
state-of-the-art auf dem neuesten Stand (der Technik) 34
stock Bestand, Vorrat 22
stranger Unbekannte(r) 11
strength Stärke 27
sturdy robust 34
subject line (Brief:) Betreffzeile 21
subsidiary Tochtergesellschaft 29
success Erfolg 36
suitable geeignet, passend 18
sum Betrag 23
summary Zusammenfassung 33
supervisor Leiter(in), Kontrolleur(in) 27
supplier Lieferant 12
supply from stock ab Lager liefern 21
to support unterstützen 15
surplus überschüssig 37
to swap tauschen 15

T

task Aufgabe 14
technician Techniker(in) 37
tension Spannung 30
terms of payment Zahlungsbedingungen 21
theoretical theoretisch 26
timber Holz, Bauholz 35
time-consuming zeitraubend 20
tip Trinkgeld 31
tool Werkzeug 12
trade fair Messe 9
trade show Messe 35
trainee Auszubildende(r) 29
trivial unwichtig 30
truth Wahrheit 27

U

uneasiness Unbehagen 30
unsatisfactory unbefriedigend, ungenügend, unzureichend 37
upset verärgert 11
user-friendly benutzerfreundlich 34
usual gewöhnlich, üblich, normal 11

V

valid gültig 25
valuable (*hier:*) wichtig 19
varnish Lack 35
to vibrate vibrieren 14
visual aids Anschauungsmaterial, visuelle Hilfen 33

W

to waste time Zeit verschwenden 11
well-done (Steak) gut durchgebraten 31
whereas während 18
willing to learn lernbereit, lernwillig 25
working atmosphere Arbeitsklima 25
working day Werktag 22
workpiece Werkstück 14
workshop Werkstatt 20

Bildquellenverzeichnis

4 iStockphoto (Helder Almeida), Calgary, Alberta; 4 PantherMedia GmbH (Benis Arapovic), München; 4 iStockphoto (Sergiy Tryapitsyn), Calgary, Alberta; 4 Fotolia.com (areafoto), New York; 5 iStockphoto (Pixsooz), Calgary, Alberta; 5 iStockphoto (kali9), Calgary, Alberta; 5 iStockphoto (Clerkenwell_Images), Calgary, Alberta; 5 Thinkstock (Monkey Business), München; 6 LinguaTV GmbH, Berlin; 6 Video(s) supplied by BBC Motion Gallery, London; 6 ZDF, Mainz; 6 ZDF Enterprises GmbH, Mainz; 8 iStockphoto (Helder Almeida), Calgary, Alberta; 8 iStockphoto (kristian sekulic), Calgary, Alberta; 8 iStockphoto (Aldo Murillo), Calgary, Alberta; 8 iStockphoto (daniel rodriguez), Calgary, Alberta; 11 iStockphoto (4x6), Calgary, Alberta; 12 Fotolia.com (areafoto), New York; 12 iStockphoto (Dmitry Kalinovsky), Calgary, Alberta; 12 Thinkstock (Goodshoot), München; 12 iStockphoto (fstop123), Calgary, Alberta; 14 shutterstock (Dmitry Kalinovsky), New York, NY; 15 iStockphoto (mediaphotos), Calgary, Alberta; 16 iStockphoto (Bart Coenders), Calgary, Alberta; 16 iStockphoto (gpointstudio), Calgary, Alberta; 16 iStockphoto (nolimitpictures), Calgary, Alberta; 16 PantherMedia GmbH (Benis Arapovic), München; 18 iStockphoto (PeskyMonkey), Calgary, Alberta; 20 iStockphoto (Warwick Lister-Kaye), Calgary, Alberta; 20 iStockphoto (Sergiy Tryapitsyn), Calgary, Alberta; 20 iStockphoto (TommL), Calgary, Alberta; 20 iStockphoto (andres balcazar), Calgary, Alberta; 24 iStockphoto (dra_schwartz), Calgary, Alberta; 24 iStockphoto (Alex), Calgary, Alberta; 24 iStockphoto (Don Bayley), Calgary, Alberta; 24 iStockphoto (Pixsooz), Calgary, Alberta; 26 Thinkstock (Wavebreak Media), München; 28 dreamstime.com (Diego Vito Cervo), Brentwood, TN; 28 iStockphoto (kali9), Calgary, Alberta; 28 iStockphoto (Clerkenwell_Images), Calgary, Alberta; 28 Thinkstock (Purestock), München; 29 Thinkstock (BananaStock), München; 30 Thinkstock (Stockbyte), München; 31 iStockphoto (kristian sekulic), Calgary, Alberta; 32 iStockphoto (Scott Feuer), Calgary, Alberta; 32 iStockphoto (poba), Calgary, Alberta; 32 iStockphoto (Clerkenwell_Images), Calgary, Alberta; 32 shutterstock (wavebreakmedia ltd), New York, NY; 33 shutterstock (MJTH), New York, NY; 35 iStockphoto (Joshua Hodge Photography), Calgary, Alberta; 36 iStockphoto (Claudia Dewald), Calgary, Alberta; 36 iStockphoto (YinYang), Calgary, Alberta; 36 Thinkstock (Monkey Business), München; 36 iStockphoto (Steve Debenport), Calgary, Alberta; 37 iStockphoto (Sean Locke), Calgary, Alberta; 40 LinguaTV GmbH, Berlin; 41 LinguaTV GmbH, Berlin; 42 ZDF Enterprises GmbH, Mainz; 43 ZDF Enterprises GmbH, Mainz; 44 ZDF, Mainz; 44 ZDF Enterprises GmbH, Mainz; 45 Video(s) supplied by BBC Motion Gallery, London; 93 JupiterImages photos.com, Tucson, AZ; **COVER** iStockphoto (sturti), Calgary, Alberta; **COVER** iStockphoto (Bob Dorn), Calgary, Alberta

Sollte es in einem Einzelfall nicht gelungen sein, den korrekten Rechteinhaber ausfindig zu machen, so werden berechtigte Ansprüche selbstverständlich im Rahmen der üblichen Regelungen abgegolten.

Further reading

The Internet and intercultural communication

R — Read the following text and answer the questions below.

The Internet and intercultural awareness

Whether right or wrong, globalization, as one writer puts it sounds unstoppable. Mass tourism, the interdependency of world markets and the Internet with its cheap and instant links to even the remotest
5 corners of the globe have all contributed to an upgrowth in intercultural communication. In the course of their daily working lives more and more people over the world are confronted with the task of communicating with people from cultures very different from their own. English, often not native to either speaker, is most frequently the
10 language employed on the Internet, i.e. the lingua franca. Yet the language itself is almost the least of it; intercultural awareness and tolerance play a central role in making global communication work. How we express our needs, desires and feelings, however, is determined by the cultural context in which we operate. Caution is called for,
15 though, in jumping to the conclusion that certain behavior is typically American, Malaysian or Swedish. We should also be aware that age, sex, regional differences, economic status and just plain personality differences also influence our communication patterns.
Certain core competences such as open-mindedness, respect, flexibility,
20 and the ability to tolerate different habits can facilitate intercultural communication. More specifically, awareness and respect for the cultural differences in such areas as degree of formality, styles of addressing your counterpart, and time-management are helpful.

Appendix | Further reading

1. Does everyone agree on the import of globalization? If not, how do opinions differ? What do you, personally, think?
2. What factors have played a role in the spread of international contacts between people? What are the consequences? And for you personally?
3. What is meant by the term lingua franca?
4. Aside from being able to speak the other person's language, what do you need in order to deal with foreigners? Can you think of one example?
5. What factors determine how we speak to other people?
6. What makes it easier to talk to people from other parts of the world?
7. Can you think of any ways in which formality or style of address might differ from one country to the other?
8. In what way does the Internet influence intercultural communication?

United Kingdom

Maps | United Kingdom, USA

USA

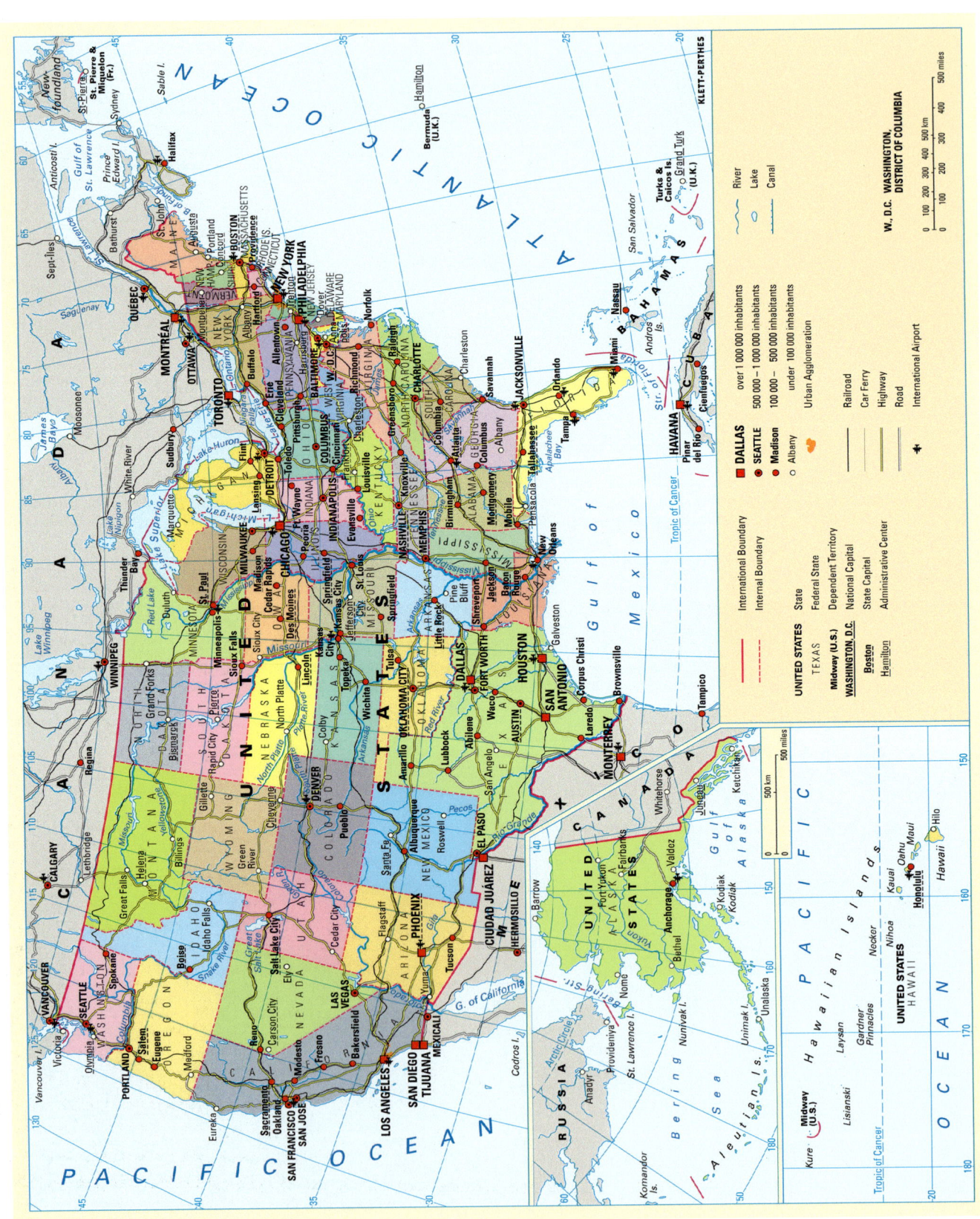